A BOOK OF JEWISH THOUGHTS

THE CHIEF RABBI DR JOSEPH H. HERTZ

Alicia Editions

BEHOLD, the days come, saith the Lord God, that I will send a famine in the land, not a famine of bread, nor a thirst for water, but of hearing the words of the Lord.

AMOS 8. 11.

Table des matières

Partie II

THE PEOPLE OF THE BOOK

Partie III

THE TESTIMONY OF THE NATIONS

Partie IV

THE VOICE OF PRAYER (THE JEWISH YEAR)

Partie V

THE VOICE OF WISDOM

PREFATORY NOTE

THIS Book of Jewish Thoughts brings the message of Judaism together with memories of Jewish martyrdom and spiritual achievement throughout the ages. Its first part, 'I am an Hebrew', covers the more important aspects of the life and consciousness of the Jew. The second, 'The People of the Book', deals with Israel's religious contribution to mankind, and touches upon some epochal events in Israel's story. In the third, 'The Testimony of the Nations', will be found some striking tributes to Jews and Judaism from non-Jewish sources. The fourth part, 'The Voice of Prayer', surveys the Sacred Occasions of the Jewish Year, and takes note of their echoes in the Liturgy. The fifth and concluding part, 'The Voice of Wisdom', is, in the main, a collection of the deep sayings of the Jewish sages on the ultimate problems of Life and the Hereafter.

The nucleus from which this Jewish anthology gradually developed was produced three years ago for the use of Jewish sailors and soldiers. To many of them, I have been assured, it came as a re-discovery of the imperishable wealth of Israel's heritage; while to the non-Jew into whose hands it fell it was a striking revelation of Jewish ideals and teachings. I can pray for no better result for this enlarged Library Edition.

Grateful acknowledgement is due to the authors, translators, and publishers, for their courteous permission to reprint selections from

1

their works; to Dayan H. M. Lazarus, M.A., and Miss Elsa Linde, for various useful suggestions; and to the Revs. J. Mann, D.Litt., S. Lipson, and I. Livingstone for help in the preparation of the Index of Subjects.

J. H. H.
London, 1920.

PARTIE I

I AM AN HEBREW

THEN said they unto him, Tell us, we pray thee, ... what is thine occupation? and whence comest thou? what is thy country? and of what people art thou?

And he said unto them, I am an Hebrew; and I fear the Lord, the God of heaven, which hath made the sea and the dry land.

JONAH 1. 8, 9.

YE ARE MY WITNESSES

אַתֶּם עֵדַי

YE are My witnesses, saith the Lord, and My servant whom I have chosen.

ISAIAH 43. 10.

THE history of Israel is the great living proof of the working of Divine Providence in the affairs of the world. Alone among the nations, Israel has shared in all great movements since mankind became conscious of their destinies. If there is no Divine purpose in the long travail of Israel, it is vain to seek for any such purpose in man's life. In the reflected light of that purpose each Jew should lead his life with an added dignity.

JOSEPH JACOBS, 1897.

EVERY Hebrew should look upon his Faith as a temple extending over every land to prove the immutability of God and the unity of His

5

purposes. He should regard himself as one of the pillars which support that temple from falling to the ground; and add, however insignificant in itself, to the strength, the durability, and the beauty of the whole.

GRACE AGUILAR, 1842.

I AM AN HEBREW

I WILL continue to hold my banner aloft. I find myself born—ay, born—into a people and a religion. The preservation of my people must be for a purpose, for God does nothing without a purpose. His reasons are unfathomable to me, but on my own reason I place little dependence; test it where I will it fails me. The simple, the ultimate in every direction is sealed to me. It is as difficult to understand matter as mind. The courses of the planets are no harder to explain than the growth of a blade of grass. Therefore am I willing to remain a link in the great chain. What has been preserved for four thousand years was not saved that I should overthrow it. My people have survived the prehistoric paganism, the Babylonian polytheism, the aesthetic Hellenism, the sagacious Romanism, at once the blandishments and persecutions of the Church; and it will survive the modern dilettantism and the current materialism, holding aloft the traditional Jewish ideals inflexibly until the world shall become capable of recognizing their worth.

CYRUS ADLER, 1894.

THE GOOD FIGHT

F thou hadst lived in the dread days of martyrdom, and the peoples had fallen on thee to force thee to apostatize from thy faith, thou wouldst surely, as did so many, have given thy life in its defence. Well then, fight now the fight laid on thee in the better days, the fight with evil desire; fight and conquer, and seek for allies in this warfare of your soul, seek them in the fear of God and the study of the Law. Forget not that God recompenses according to the measure wherewith ye withstand the evil in your heart. Be a man in thy youth; but if thou wert then defeated in the struggle, return, return at last to God, however old thou mayest be.

ELEAZAR (ROKËACH) OF WORMS, *c.* 1200. (*Trans. M. Joseph.*)

EVERY ISRAELITE HOLDS THE HONOUR OF HIS ENTIRE PEOPLE IN HIS HANDS

I

'ALL Israelites are mutually accountable for each other.' In a boat at sea one of the men began to bore a hole in the bottom of the boat. On being remonstrated with, he answered: 'I am only boring under my own seat'. 'Yes', said his comrades, 'but when the sea rushes in we shall all be drowned with you.' So it is with Israel. Its weal or its woe is in the hands of every individual Israelite.

TALMUD.

II

WE Jews have a more pressing responsibility for our lives and beliefs than perhaps any other religious community.

Don't shelter yourself in any course of action by the idea that 'it is *my* affair'. It is your affair, but it is also mine and the community's. Nor can we neglect the world beyond. A fierce light beats upon the Jew. It is a grave responsibility this—to be a Jew; and you can't escape from it, even if you choose to ignore it. Ethically or religiously, we Jews can be and do nothing light-heartedly. Ten bad Jews may help to damn us; ten good Jews may help to save us. Which *minyan* will you join?

C. G. MONTEFIORE, 1900.

THE PATHS OF LIFE

I

MY son, give God all honour and the gratitude which is His due. Thou hast need of Him, but He needs thee not. Put no trust in thy mere corporeal well-being here below. Many a one has lain down to sleep at nightfall, but at morn has not risen again. Fear the Lord, the God of thy fathers; fail never at eventide to pronounce the great word wherein Israel is wont to proclaim that He is, and that He is One, and One only; at dawn fail never to read the appointed prayer. See that thou guard well thy soul's holiness; let the thought of thy heart be saintly, and profane not thy soul with words of impurity.

Visit the sick and suffering man, and let thy countenance be cheerful when he sees it, but not so that thou oppress the helpless one with gaiety. Comfort those that are in grief; let piety where thou seest it affect thee even to tears; and then it may be that thou wilt be spared the grief of weeping over the death of thy children.

Respect the poor man by gifts whose hand he knows not of; be not deaf to his beseechings, deal not hard words out to him, and give him of thy richest food when he sits at meat with thee.

From a wicked neighbour, see that thou keep aloof, and spend not much of thy time among the people who speak ill of their brother-man;

be not as the fly that is always seeking sick and wounded places; and tell not of the faults and failings of those about thee.

Take no one to wife unworthy to be thy life's partner, and keep thy sons close to the study of Divine things. Dare not to rejoice when thine enemy comes to the ground; but give him food when he hungers. Be on thy guard lest thou give pain ever to the widow and the orphan; and beware lest thou ever set thyself up to be both witness and judge against an other.

Never enter thy house with abrupt and startling step, and bear not thyself so that those who dwell under thy roof shall dread when in thy presence. Purge thy soul of angry passion, that inheritance of fools; love wise men, and strive to know more and more of the works and the ways of the Creator.

ELIEZER BEN ISAAC, 1050.

II

BE not ready to quarrel; avoid oaths and passionate adjurations, excess of laughter and outbursts of wrath; they disturb and confound the reason of man. Avoid all dealings wherein there is a lie; utter not the name of God superfluously, or in places dirty or defiled.

Cut from under thee all mere human supports, and make not gold the foremost longing of thy life; for that is the first step to idolatry. Rather give money than words; and as to ill words, see that thou place them in the scale of understanding before they leave thy lips.

What has been uttered in thy presence, even though not told as secret, let it not pass from thee to others. And if one tell thee a tale, say not to him that thou hast heard it all before. Do not fix thine eyes too much on one who is far above thee in wealth, but on those who are behind thee in worldly fortune.

Put no one to open shame; misuse not thy power against any one; who can tell whether thou wilt not some day be powerless thyself?

Do not struggle vaingloriously for the small triumph of showing thyself in the right and a wise man in the wrong; thou art not one whit the wiser therefor. Be not angry or unkind to any one for trifles, lest thou make thyself enemies unnecessarily.

Do not refuse things out of mere obstinacy to thy fellow-citizens, rather put thy will below their wishes. Avoid, as much as may be, bad men, men of persistent angry feelings, fools; thou canst get nothing from their company but shame. Be the first to extend courteous greeting to every one, whatever be his faith; provoke not to wrath one of another belief than thine.

ASHER BEN YECHIEL, 1300.

IN THE OLD GHETTO

I N the narrow lanes and by-ways of the old Jewish quarter of many
a European town there grew up that beautiful Jewish home-life
which, though its story is seldom recorded, is more important than the
outer events and misfortunes that historians have made note of. And as
we look upon the unsightly houses, the wretched exterior seems to
float away and the home-scenes of joy and love and religious
constancy shine brilliantly forth—perpetual lamps—and explain how,
in spite of woe and misery such as have fallen to the lot of no other
people, the Jews have found strength to live and hope on.

    D. PHILIPSON, 1894.

SAY what you will of the Judaism of the Middle Ages; call it narrow;
deride it as superstitious; unless lost to all sense of justice, or without
power to dive beneath the surface of the seeming to the roots of the
real, you cannot but witness to the incontrovertible fact that for sweet-
ness and spirituality of life, the Jew of the Ghetto, the Jew of the
Middle Ages, the Jew under the yoke of the Talmud, challenges the
whole world.

    E. G. HIRSCH, 1895.

THE JEWISH WOMAN

I N the days of horror of the later Roman Empire, throughout the time of the migration of nations, it was not war alone that destroyed and annihilated all those peoples of which, despite their former world-dominating greatness, nothing remains but their name. It was rather the ensuing demoralization of home life. This is proved—it cannot be repeated too often—by the Jews; for they suffered more severely and more cruelly by wars than any other nation; but, among them, the inmost living germ of morality—strict discipline and family devotion —was at all times preserved. This wonderful and mysterious preservation of the Jewish people is due to the Jewish woman. This is her glory, not alone in the history of her own people, but in the history of the world.

M. LAZARUS.

THE Jew's home has rarely been his 'castle'. Throughout the ages it has been something far higher—his sanctuary.

J. H. HERTZ.

BE careful not to cause woman to weep, for God counts her tears.

Israel was redeemed from Egypt on account of the virtue of its women. He who weds a good woman, it is as if he had fulfilled all the precepts of the Law.

TALMUD.

THE JEWISH MOTHER

JEWISH custom bids the Jewish mother, after her preparations for the Sabbath have been completed on Friday evening, kindle the Sabbath lamp. That is symbolic of the Jewish woman's influence on her own home, and through it upon larger circles. She is the inspirer of a pure, chaste, family life whose hallowing influences are incalculable; she is the centre of all spiritual endeavours, the confidante and fosterer of every undertaking. To her the Talmudic sentence applies: 'It is woman alone through whom God's blessings are vouchsafed to a house'.

HENRIETTA SZOLD, 1893.

YIDDISH CRADLE SONG

O! HUSH thee, my darling, sleep soundly my son,
Sleep soundly and sweetly till day has begun;
For under the bed of good children at night
There lies, till the morning, a kid snowy white.
We'll send it to market to buy *Sechora*,
While my little lad goes to study Torah.
Sleep soundly at night and learn Torah by day,
Then thou'll be a Rabbi when I have grown grey.

But I'll give thee to-morrow ripe nuts and a toy,
If thou'lt sleep as I bid thee, my own little boy.
(*Trans. Alice Lucas.*)

RELIGIOUS EDUCATION

I T seems to me that if the development of the religious sense is omitted from education, the most exalted idea of goodness is left out. Life is so much the poorer for being shorn of the halo of high spiritual aspiration. Instead of a fixed and lofty ideal of life and conduct, based on the highest conception of Divine Perfection of which the human mind is capable, there prevails a limited and *fluctuating* ideal, subject to the chance influences of surroundings and associates, and coloured by the social grade and worldly interests of each individual.

JULIA M. COHEN, 1907.

THE thread on which the different good qualities of human beings are strung as pearls, is the fear of God. When the fastenings of this fear are unloosed, the pearls roll in all directions and are lost one by one.

BOOK OF MORALS, 15th cent.

THE knowledge of Hebrew is the golden hinge upon which our national and religious existence turns. Flowing down from the hills of eternity, the Hebrew language has been set apart by God as the receptacle of truths destined to sway mankind and humanize the world.

SABATO MORAIS, 1876.

THE SACRED TONGUE

THE Synagogue service is essentially the expression of the soul of collective Israel. In the Synagogue we meet as Jews, there in prayer, in aspiration, in confession of faith, to carry on the stream of spiritual effort which has flowed unbroken through the ages ever since Israel became conscious of himself. Therefore the prayers will not merely voice private needs and modern ideas, but will chiefly speak of Israel. And so they will largely be in Hebrew, Israel's historic language. You may get rid of Hebrew, but with it you will get rid of the Synagogue too, of the Synagogue as a living organism, as the well-spring of Jewish feeling and the inspiration of Jewish life. Nor is this all. The claim of Hebrew, though bound up with the interests of public worship, yet transcends them. It will meet you whenever you open your Jewish history, whenever you open your Bible. As long as we remain Jews and call the Bible our own, the Tongue in which it is written must be inestimably sacred to us.

MORRIS JOSEPH, 1907.

THE HEBREW LANGUAGE

T HE Hebrew language is the great depository of all that is best in the soul-life of the Congregation of Israel. Without it we will become severed from the great Tree which is life unto those that cling to it. Hellenistic Judaism[1] is the only one known to history which dared to make this experiment of dispensing with the Sacred Language. The result was death. It withered away and terminated in total and whole-sale apostasy from Judaism. Let us not deceive ourselves. There is no future in this country for a Judaism that resists either the English or the Hebrew language.

    S. SCHECHTER, 1904.

THERE is a vast storehouse filled with treasures. The key, the Hebrew language, is in our guardianship. Have we a right to throw the key into the ocean of oblivion? More than that: when we have ceased to be efficient guardians of our treasures, of what use are we in the world? I fear that in the case of such flagrant dereliction of duty, the twentieth century will have in store for us not a Ghetto, but a grave.

    HENRIETTA SZOLD, 1896.

---

1. The Greek-speaking Jewish communities of antiquity, especially Alexandria.

WHAT IS CULTURE?

NOT what a man has—knowledge, skill, or goods of life—determines his culture, but what a man *is*: culture is not so much mastery of things as mastery of self. And only that nation can be called cultured which adds to or, at least, broadens and deepens the spiritual assets of mankind; which introduces some distinctive note into the soul-life of the world; which teaches humanity a new angle of vision towards the Infinite; and by its living and, if need be, by its dying, vindicates the eternal values of life—conscience, honour, liberty.

Judged by this test, some of the littlest of peoples—Judea, Greece, Elizabethan England—stand foremost among cultured nations, champions of the sacred heritage of man. Judged by this test, many a poor Jew, though he be devoid of the graces, amenities, and comforts of life, is yet possessed of culture. An ancient language, a classical language, a holy language, is as familiar to him as his mother-tongue; saturated is he with the sublimest of literatures, which hallows his life and endows him with high faith and invincible courage.

Sympathetic appreciation of this indomitable type, this harmonious albeit rugged personality, might well be taken as a touchstone of a man's mentality, culture, and humanity.

J. H. HERTZ, 1915.

THE STUDENT OF
THE TORAH

I F one asks a student to-day why he studies, he will at once, in spite
of his youth, give a very practical answer. He mentions the profession for which he is preparing himself, and through which he will
obtain a lucrative office or a comfortable position in life.

It is entirely different with those who expended their time and
powers on the study of the Talmud. They wished to derive no profit
from their studies; not to use them, as a Mishna teacher says, 'as a
spade to dig wherewith nor as a crown wherewith to aggrandise
oneself'. 'Say not', exclaims the Talmud, 'I will study the Torah in
order that people may call me Sage or Master, but study from pure love
to God, to cleave more closely unto Him through the knowledge and
understanding of His word.' Day and night did they bury themselves in
the study of subjects that had nothing to do with social life or with
gain; often they became engrossed in the investigation of laws of sacrifices and purification, although these had long since grown obsolete.
They desired nothing but knowledge, understanding, illumination.
Where is there another people on earth among whom studies which
aimed only at truth and the development of the spiritual life were culti-
vated with such pure, devoted, and selfless love as in Israel?

A. JELLINEK, 1882.

BAR MITZVAH PRAYER

1

O MY God, and God of My Fathers,

On this solemn and sacred day, which marketh my passage from boyhood to manhood, I humbly venture to raise my eyes unto Thee, and to declare with sincerity and truth that henceforth I will observe all Thy commandments, and undertake to bear the responsibility of all mine actions towards Thee. In my earliest infancy I was brought within Thy sacred covenant with Israel, and to-day I again enter as an active responsible member the pale of Thine elect congregation, in the midst of which I will never cease to glorify Thy holy name in the face of all nations.

Do Thou, O Heavenly Father, hearken unto this my humble prayer, and vouchsafe unto me Thy gracious blessings, so that my earthly life may be sustained and made happy by Thine ineffable mercies. Teach me the way of Thy statutes, that I may obey them, and faithfully carry out Thy ordinances. Dispose my heart to love Thee and to fear Thy holy name, and grant me Thy support and the strength necessary to avoid the worldly dangers which encompass the path lying before me. Save me from temptation, so that I may with fortitude observe Thy holy Law and those precepts on which human happiness and eternal life depend. Thus I will every day of my life trustfully and gladly proclaim: 'Hear, O Israel, the Lord is our God, the Lord is one!'

BENJAMIN ARTOM, 1868.

---

1. In use in English Sephardi Congregations on the occasion of a lad reaching the age of thirteen—his religious majority (Bar Mitzvah).

ON THE THRESHOLD OF MANHOOD

M Y son, keep the commandment of thy father,
    And forsake not the teaching of thy mother.
Bind them continually upon thy heart,
Tie them about thy neck.
When thou walkest, it shall lead thee;
When thou liest down, it shall watch over thee;
And when thou awakest, it shall talk with thee.
For the commandment is a lamp, and the teaching is light,
And reproofs of instruction are the way of life:
To keep thee from the evil woman.
PROVERBS 6. 20-4.

RABBI Hanina[1], son of Dosa, said: 'He in whom the fear of sin comes before wisdom, his wisdom shall endure; but he in whom wisdom comes before the fear of sin, his wisdom will not endure.'

Rabbi Eleazar[2], son of Azaryah, said: 'He whose wisdom exceeds his works, to what is he like? To a tree whose branches are many, but whose roots are few; and the wind comes and plucks it up and overturns it upon its face. But he whose works exceed his wisdom, to what is he like? To a tree whose branches are few, but whose roots are many, so that even if all the winds in the world come and blow upon it, it cannot be stirred from its place.'

ETHICS OF THE FATHERS.

---

1. Lived about 10 B.C.E.-90 C.E. See p. 292.
2. Lived first century; President of the Academy at Yabneh.

A FATHER'S ADMONITION

FEAR the Lord the God of thy Fathers and serve Him in love, for fear only restrains a man from sin, while love stimulates him to good. Accustom thyself to habitual goodness, for a man's character is what habit makes it. The perfection of the body is a necessary antecedent to the perfection of the soul, for health is the key to the inner chamber. Measure thy words, for by multiplying words thou increasest error. If thou find in the Law or the Prophets or the Sages a hard saying which thou canst not understand, stand fast by thy faith and attribute the fault to thine own want of intelligence. Place it in a corner of your heart for future consideration, but despise not thy religion because thou art unable to understand one difficult matter.

Love truth and uprightness—the ornaments of the soul—and cleave unto them; prosperity so obtained is built on a sure rock. Keep firmly to thy word; let not a legal contract or witnesses be more binding than thine verbal promise whether in public or in private. Disdain reservations and subterfuges, evasions and sharp practices. Woe to him who builds his house upon them. Abhor inactivity and indolence, the causes of destruction of body, of penury, of self-contempt—the ladders of Satan and his satellites.

Defile not your souls by quarrelsomeness and petulance. I have seen the white become black, the low brought still lower, families

29

driven into exile, princes deposed from their high estate, great cities laid in ruins, assemblies dispersed, the pious humiliated, the honourable held lightly and despised, all on account of quarrelsomeness. Glory in forbearance, for in that is true strength and victory.

MOSES MAIMONIDES.

WHAT MAKES A MAN
A JEW?

J UDAISM is something more than a badge, something more than a
birth-mark; it is a life. To be born a Jew does not declare any of us
to be of the elect; it only designates us for enrolment among the
elect. God signs the covenant, but we have to seal it—to seal it by a life
of service. 'What makes a man a Jew?' is a question that is often asked.
The answer is, two things: membership of the Jewish brotherhood, and
loyal fulfilment of the obligations which that membership imposes. To
be of the Jewish race but to trample upon Jewish duty is to be faithless
to Israel.

MORRIS JOSEPH, 1903.

'I BELIEVE'

I BELIEVE in God, the One and Holy, the Creator and Sustainer of the world.

I believe that man possesses a Divine power wherewith he may subdue his evil impulses and passions, strive to come nearer and nearer the perfection of God, and commune with Him in prayer.

I believe that select individuals are, from time to time, called by God as prophets and charged with the mission of declaring His will unto men.

I believe that man is subject to God's law and responsible to the Searcher of the human heart and the Righteous Judge for all his thoughts and deeds.

I believe that he who confesses his sins and turns from his evil ways and truly repents is lovingly forgiven by his Father in Heaven.

I believe that the pious who obey God's law and do His will with a perfect heart, and those who truly repent, share, as immortal souls, in the everlasting life of God.

I believe that Israel was chosen by God as His anointed servant to proclaim unto the families of mankind His truth; and, though despised and rejected by men, to continue as His witness until there come in through him the Kingdom of Peace and moral perfection, and the fullness of the knowledge of God, the true Community of the Children of the living God.

M. L. MARGOLIS, 1904.

JUDAISM A POSITIVE
RELIGION

S ATISFYING the needs of anybody and everybody, of every moment and every fleeting season, is not the highest ideal which Judaism set before itself. Altogether I venture to think that the now fashionable test of determining the worth of a religion by its capability to supply the various demands of the great market of believers has something low and mercenary about it. True religion is not a jack-of-all-trades, meaning Monotheism to the philosopher, Pluralism to the crowd, some mysterious Nothing to the agnostic, Pantheism to the poet, and Service of Man to the hero-worshipper. Its mission is just as much to teach the world that there *are* false gods and false ideals as to bring it nearer to the true one. Abraham, the friend of God, who was destined to become the first winner of souls, began his career, according to the legend, with breaking idols, and it is his particular glory to have been in opposition to the whole world. Judaism means to convert the world, not to convert itself. It will not die in order *not* to live. It disdains a victory by defeating itself, in giving up its essential doctrines, its most sacred symbols, its most precious traditions, and its most vital teaching. It has confidence in the world; it hopes and prays and waits patiently for the Great Day when the world will be ripe for its acceptance.

S. SCHECHTER, 1893.

THE MISSION OF ISRAEL

T hink of the meaning of that simple ceremony in our service when the Minister takes his stand before the Ark, and clasping the sacred scroll in his arms, proclaims the שמע, belief in the unity of One Eternal, Almighty God. This rite symbolizes the mission of Israel to the world: With the Law of God folded in his arms and its words engraved upon his heart, he has gone up and down the earth proclaiming his belief in the One Supreme Being—a Being whose spirit fills all time and all space, a Being never embodied, but made manifest to man in the glory of the creation and in His all-wise behests, which teach mercy, love, and justice....

HERMANN ADLER, 1895.

A CLEAR and concise definition of Judaism[1] is very difficult to give, for the reason that it is not a religion pure and simple based upon accepted creeds, but is one inseparably connected with the Jewish nation as the depositary and guardian of the truths held by it for mankind.

Far from having become 1,900 years ago a stagnant religion, Judaism has ever remained 'a river of God full of living waters', which, while running within the river-bed of a single nation, has continued to feed anew the great streams of human civilization.

K. KOHLER, 1904.

---

1. From *The Jewish Encyclopedia*, 'Judaism' (London and New York: Funk & Wagnalls).

TOLERANCE

I

THOU art the Lord, and all beings are Thy servants, Thy domain;
    And through those who serve idols vain
Thine honour is not detracted from,
For they all aim to Thee to come;
But they are as the blind,
That seeking the royal road could not find;
The one sank in destruction's well;
Another into a cavity fell,
And all thought they had reached what they sought
Yet toiled for naught.
SOLOMON IBN GABIROL, 1050. (*Trans. M. Jastrow.*)

I CALL heaven and earth to witness that whether it be Jew or heathen,
man or woman, free or bondman—only according to their acts does the
Divine spirit rest upon them.
    MIDRASH.

SALVATION is attained not by subscription to metaphysical dogmas, but solely by love of God that fulfils itself in action. This is a cardinal truth in Judaism.

CHASDAI CRESCAS, 1410.

II

YOUR question, why I do not try to make converts, has, I must say, somewhat surprised me. The duty to proselytize springs clearly from the idea that outside a certain belief there is no salvation. I, as a Jew, am not bound to accept that dogma, because, according to the teachings of the Rabbis, *the righteous of all nations shall have part in the rewards of the future world.* Your motive, therefore, is foreign to me; nay, as a Jew, I am not allowed publicly to attack any religion which is sound in its moral teachings.

MOSES MENDELSSOHN, 1770. *To a non-Jewish correspondent.*

IAM the creature of God, and so is my fellow-man; my calling is in the town, and his in the fields; I go early to my work, and he to his; he does not boast of his labour nor I of mine, and if thou wouldst say, 'I accomplish great things and he little things', we have learnt that *whether a man accomplish great things or small, his reward is the same if only his heart be set upon Heaven.*

TALMUD.

OUR HERITAGE

O UR laws have been such as have always inspired admiration and imitation in all other men.

Nay, farther, multitudes of mankind have had a great inclination of a long time to follow our religious observances; for there is not any city of the Grecians, nor any of the barbarians, nor any nation whatsoever, whither our custom of resting on the seventh day hath not come, and by which our fasts and lighting up lamps, and many of our prohibitions as to our food, are not observed;[1] they also endeavour to imitate our mutual concord with one another, and the charitable distribution of our goods, and our diligence in our trades, and our fortitude in undergoing distresses on account of our laws. And what is here matter of the greatest admiration, our Law hath no bait of pleasure to allure men to it, but it prevails by its own force; and as God himself pervades all the world, so hath our Law passed through all the world also.

As to the laws themselves more words are unnecessary, for they are visible in their own nature, and appear to teach not impiety, but the truest piety in the world. They are enemies to injustice; they banish idleness and luxurious living; and they instruct men to be content with what they have, and to be laborious in their calling. They forbid men to make war from a desire of getting more, but make men courageous in defending the laws. On which account I am so bold as to say that we are become the teachers of other men in the greatest number of things, and those of the most excellent nature only; for what is more excellent than inviolable piety? What is more just than submission to laws, and more advantageous than mutual love and concord? And this so far that we are to be neither divided by calamities, nor to become injurious and seditious in prosperity; but to contemn death when we are in war, and in peace to apply ourselves to our handicrafts, or to our tillage of the ground; while we in all things and in all ways are satisfied that God is the Judge and Governor of our actions.

FLAVIUS JOSEPHUS, 1st cent.

---

1. From *The Jewish Encyclopedia*, 'Judaism' (London and New York: Funk & Wagnalls).

OUR FATHERS

L ET us now praise famous men,
   Our fathers in their generations.
The Lord manifested in them great glory,
Even His mighty power from the beginning.
Such as did bear rule in their kingdoms,
And were men renowned for their power,
Giving counsel by their understanding,
Such as have brought tidings in prophecies:
Leaders of the people by their counsels,
And by their understanding men of learning for the people;
Wise were their words in their instruction:
Such as sought out musical tunes,
And set forth verses in writing:
Rich men furnished with ability,
Living peaceably in their habitations:
All these were honoured in their generations,
And were a glory in their days.
There be of them, that have left a name behind them,
To declare their praises.
And some there be, which have no memorial;
Who are perished as though they had not been,
And are become as though they had not been born,

And their children after them.
But these were men of mercy,
Whose righteous deeds have not been forgotten.
With their seed shall remain continually a good inheritance;
Their children are within the covenants.
Their seed standeth fast,
And their children for their sakes.
Their seed shall remain for ever,
And their glory shall not be blotted out.
Their bodies are buried in peace,
And their name liveth for evermore.
Peoples will declare their wisdom,
And the congregation telleth out their praise.
ECCLESIASTICUS 44. 1-15.

THE OBLIGATIONS OF
HEREDITY

JEWISH history admonishes the Jews: *'Noblesse oblige'*. The privilege of belonging to a people to whom the honourable title of the 'Veteran of History' has been conceded puts serious responsibilities on your shoulders. You must demonstrate that you are worthy of your heroic past.

S. M. DUBNOW, 1893.

OUR virtues are Israel's: all our success in life we owe to the fact that the blood of the 'toughest of peoples' is coursing in our veins. Our vices are our own. Now the world inverts the distribution. Our virtues it credits to us, to our individual brilliancy, diligence, courage. Whereas the crimes, vices, and failings of any single Jew, no matter how estranged from his people or his people's faith he may be, it puts down to his Jewishness, and fathers them upon the entire Jewish race.

Is it not a matter of sacred honour, as far as in us lies to counteract the world's injustice to our people by rendering, when the opportunity is ours, some repayment for all we owe to Israel?

J. H. HERTZ, 1915.

ZEDAKAH –CHARITY

TUR, II, § 247[1]

T HE dispensing of charity according to one's means is a positive precept, which demands greater care and diligence in its fulfilment than all the other positive precepts of the Law. For its neglect may possibly lead to the taking of life, inasmuch as the denial of timely aid may compass the death of the poor man who needs our immediate help.

Whoso closes his eyes to this duty and hardens his heart to his needy brother is called a worthless man, and is regarded as an idolater. But whosoever is careful in the fulfilment of this duty attests himself as belonging to the seed of Abraham, whom the Lord hath blessed: 'For I have known him, to the end that he may command his children and his household after him, that they may keep the way of the Lord, to do *Zedakah* and justice' (Genesis 18. 19).

Charity is the main foundation of Israel's pre-eminence, and the basis of the Law of Truth. As the prophet says unto Zion: 'By *Zedakah* shalt thou be established' (Isaiah 54. 14). Its practice will alone bring about Israel's redemption: 'Zion shall be redeemed with justice, and they that return of her with *Zedakah*' (Isaiah 1. 27). Charity is greater than all sacrifices, says Rabbi Eleazar; even as it is written,

'To do *Zedakah* and justice is more acceptable to the Lord than sacrifice' (Proverbs 21. 3).

Whoso pities the poor shall himself receive compassion from the Holy One, blessed be He. Let man further reflect that as there is a wheel of fortune revolving in this world, perchance some day either he himself, or his son, or his son's son, may be brought down to the same lowly state. Nor let it enter his mind to say: 'How can I give to the poor and thus lessen my possessions?' For man must know that he is not the master of what he has, but only the guardian, to carry out the will of Him who entrusted these things to his keeping.

Whosoever withholds alms from the needy thereby withdraws himself from the lustre of the Shechinah and the light of the Law.

Let man therefore be exceedingly diligent in the right bestowal of charity.

JACOB BEN ASHER, 1320. (*Trans. A. Feldman.*)

---

1. In Hebrew there is only one word, *Zedakah*, for both Charity and Justice. Charity to the poor is thus merely justice to the poor.

ZEDAKAH –JUSTICE.

'*NEITHER shalt thou favour a poor man his cause*' (Exodus 23. 3). It is one of the deep and fundamental traits of Judaism that whilst presupposing sympathy and commiseration with the poor and the hapless, it nevertheless fears that in a suit-at-law justice might be outraged *in favour of the poor man* even when he is in the wrong—outraged just because of his very distress. Sympathy and compassion are emotions that have their proper place and use, but even these noble feelings must be silenced in the presence of Justice. In this Scriptural command there is a height of conception, a sublimity of moral view, which compels the reverence of all.

A. GEIGER, 1865.

THE JEWISH POOR

THE Kingdom of God—the Rabbis held—is inconsistent with a state of social misery. They were not satisfied with feeding the poor. Their great ideal was not to allow a man to be poor, not to allow him to come down into the depths of poverty. They say, 'Try to prevent it by teaching him a trade. Try all methods before you permit him to become an object of charity, which must degrade him, tender as your dealings with him may be.'

S. SCHECHTER, 1893.

IT is an arduous task to think for the Jewish poor. He has a rooted notion that he is the best, the only judge, of what is good for you to do for him. And the fact is that these self-confident recipients of your generosity really are often your betters in many qualifications. Large-mindedness is needed here. We must respect old habits; we must fathom the deep moral springs of life. We must beware that our brothers do not divest themselves of their best, and assume our worst.

I. ABRAHAMS, 1896.

AT 'THE OLD PEOPLE'S REST', JERUSALEM

A SCORE or so of old men with white beards seated at a long table covered by open books of the Talmud. The sacred scroll of the Law is enshrined at their left, and behind them we see ponderous old tomes, tight fitted into the alcove of a vault-like chamber, with quaint curves and angles. Is not this some souvenir from the brush of an old master? No, it is a group of inmates of the 'Old People's Rest' at Jerusalem.

What strikes one most about the inmates is the refinement and intellectuality of their features. It is a workhouse where aged failures in the struggle for existence are permitted to pass away in peace. Not here will we meet with degraded types of the European inebriate or jailbird. They are all representative of one very fascinating aspect of Judaism which it is the fashion to doubt or decry. It is not only in India that the Yogi, or contemplative Sage, is to be met with, who, having fulfilled his whole duty as a man, retires from active life to meditate on the here and the hereafter. We have our Jewish Yogis even outside the dazzling effulgence which emanates from the Zohar. They work not, neither do they spin, but the world is better for their being in it, even if not of it. It is refreshing to think that not everybody is in a hurry, not everybody busy money-making or money-spending, and that a few there are who are survivals of more tranquil ages.

E. N. ADLER, 1895.

SHARING THE BURDEN

I

W HEN trouble comes upon the congregation, it is not right for a man to say, 'I will eat and drink, and things will be peaceful for me'. Moses, our Teacher, always bore his share in the troubles of the congregation, as it is written, 'They took a stone and put it under him' (Exodus 17. 12). Could they not have given him a chair or a cushion? But then he said, 'Since the Israelites are in trouble, lo, I will bear my part with them, for he who bears his portion of the burden will live to enjoy the hour of consolation'. Woe to one who thinks, 'Ah, well, I will neglect my duty. Who can know whether I bear my part or not?' Even the stones of the house, ay, the limbs of the trees shall testify against him, as it is written, 'For the stones will cry from the wall, and the limbs of the trees will testify'.
TALMUD.

II[1]

'IT is high time', wrote Leopold Zunz, in the days when the emancipation of the Jews in Europe was being constantly postponed, or was being dealt with in a huckstering and grudging spirit, 'It is high time that instead of having rights and liberties doled out to them, they should obtain Right and Liberty.' It was well said: 'Right and Liberty' are one and indivisible, and belong to all men as such. Well, 'Right and Liberty' are ours, if any people on the face of the earth can be said to possess them. Surely we owe something to the land and the people where and among whom our lines are fallen, and of which we are an integral part. We owe it to them to take our share of the national burdens and in the national life, to seek our prosperity in theirs, to respect the law and its representatives, from the humblest officer of justice to the Sovereign upon the throne.

SIMEON SINGER, 1894.

---

1. From *Sermons* (London: Geo. Routledge & Sons).

THE DUTY OF SELF-RESPECT

NOTHING is more dangerous for a nation or for an individual than to plead guilty to imaginary sins. Where the sin is real—by honest endeavour the sinner can purify himself. But when a man has been persuaded to suspect himself unjustly—what *can* he do? Our greatest need is emancipation from self-contempt, from this idea that we are really worse than all the world. Otherwise we may in course of time become in reality what we now imagine ourselves to be.

ACHAD HA'AM, 1891.

ANTI-SEMITISM

I

JEWISH misery has two forms, the material and the moral. In Eastern Europe, in those regions which shelter the vast majority of our race, we see a painful fight for the maintenance of a bare existence. In Western Europe, the Jew has bread; but man does not live on bread alone. His misery is moral. It exists in the constant wounding of self-respect and honour.

MAX NORDAU, 1897.

I REMEMBER when I used to come home from the Cheder[1], bleeding and crying from the wounds inflicted upon me by the Christian boys, my father used to say, 'My child, we are in Golus (exile), and we must submit to God's will'. And he made me understand that this is only a passing stage in history, as we Jews belong to Eternity, when God will comfort His people. Thus the pain was only physical; but my real suffering began later in life, when I emigrated from Roumania to so-called civilized countries, and found there what I might call the Higher Anti-Semitism, which burns the soul though it leaves the body unhurt.

S. SCHECHTER, 1903.

II

NOT rarely a Jew is heard to murmur that we must learn from our enemies and try to remedy our failings. He forgets, however, that the anti-Semitic accusations are valueless, because they are not based on a criticism of real facts, but are merely due to the psychological law according to which children, savages, and malevolent fools make persons and things against which they have an aversion responsible for their sufferings.

Pretexts change, but the hatred remains. The Jews are not hated because they have evil qualities; evil qualities are sought for in them because they are hated.

MAX NORDAU.

MY grandmother, the beautiful daughter of a family who had suffered much from persecution, had imbibed that dislike for her race which the vain are too apt to adopt when they find they are born to public contempt. The indignant feeling that should be reserved for the perse-cutor, in the mortification of their disturbed sensibility, is too often visited on the victim; and the cause of annoyance is recognized not in the ignorant malevolence of the powerful, but in the conscientious conviction of the innocent sufferer.

BENJAMIN DISRAELI, 1848.

III

ANTI-SEMITES accuse the Jewish people of an incapacity for forgi-veness and love. Let these preachers of love first practise it. Let them refrain, at least, from incendiary slanders against Israel who, among all the peoples of the world, has agonized and suffered most from hatred, malice, and all uncharitableness at the hands of others. Let such prea-chers of love remember the Mosaic Law: 'Thou shalt not bear false witness against thy neighbour'.

J. H. HERTZ, 1919.

NOT one man alone has risen up against us to destroy us, but in every generation there rise up against us those who seek to destroy us; but the Holy One, blessed be He, delivers us from their hands.

    PASSOVER HAGADAH.

NO weapon that is formed against thee shall prosper; and every tongue that shall rise against thee in judgement thou shalt condemn.

    ISAIAH 54. 17.

---

1. School, usually for religious instruction only.

THE JEW AS A PATRIOT

E VERY student of the Hebrew language is aware that we have in the conjugation of its verbs a mood known as the Intensive (Piel) Voice, which by means of an almost imperceptible modification of vowel points intensifies the meaning of the primitive root. A similar significance seems to attach to the Jews themselves in connexion with the people among whom they dwell. They are the *intensive form* of any nationality whose language and customs they adopt.
　　EMMA LAZARUS, 1882.

LOYALTY to the flag for which the sun once stood still, can only deepen our devotion to the flag on which the sun never sets.
　　Col. A. E. GOLDSMID, 1902.

THE JEWISH SOLDIER

MOTHER England, Mother England, 'mid the thousands
    Far beyond the sea to-day,
Doing battle for thy honour, for thy glory,
Is there place for us, a little band of brothers?
England, say!
Long ago and far away, O Mother England,
We were warriors brave and bold;
But a hundred nations rose in arms against us,
And the shades of exile closed o'er those heroic
Days of old.
Thou hast given us home and freedom, Mother England,
Thou hast let us live again,
Free and fearless, 'midst thy free and fearless children,
Sharing with them, as one people, grief and gladness,
Joy and pain.
For the Jew has heart and hand, our Mother England,
And they both are thine to-day—
Thine for life and thine for death—yea, thine for ever!
Wilt thou take them as we give them, freely, gladly?
England, say!
ALICE LUCAS, 1899.

THE JEW'S LOVE
OF BRITAIN

1

IS it a matter of surprise that so goodly a number of our brethren offered themselves willingly among the people? One of the master-pieces of eloquence bequeathed to us by classic antiquity is the funeral oration delivered by Pericles on those who had fallen in the Peloponne-sian War. He dilates upon the sources of Athens' greatness. He portrays in glowing colours how justice is there equally meted out to all citi-zens, from the highest to the lowest, how all are under the aegis of freedom, and all equally inspired by obedience to law. And he conti-nues: 'Such a country well deserves that her children should die for her!' The members of the House of Israel have always faithfully served the country of their birth or their adoption. But surely England deserves that we, her Jewish children, should gladly live and die for her: since here, as in no other country, the teachings of Holy Writ are venerated and obeyed. Here, as in no other Empire in the world, there breathes a passionate love of freedom, a burning hatred of tyrant wrong.

HERMANN ADLER, *at the unveiling of the Memorial to the Jewish soldiers who fell in the South African War*, 1905.

---

1. From *Anglo-Jewish Memories* (London: Geo. Routledge & Sons).

57

TO ENGLAND

LINES OF A RUSSIAN JEW
IN childhood I learned to love thee,
Thy name was a legend to me;
I dreamt of a distant great island,
Where men may be strong, yet be free.
And I, who the clatter of fetters
Have heard in my childhood and youth,
Do bless thee for giving me refuge,
And faith in the triumph of truth.
Thou art not my stepmother, England,
My sister of mercy thou art;
For thee in the hour of thy trial
A brotherly love fills my heart.
P. M. RASKIN, 1914.

JUDAISM AND THE JEW
IN AMERICA

I

L IKE the river that takes its rise in the distant hills, gradually courses its way through the country, passing alike through sublime landscape and hideous morass, offering its banks for the foundation of great cities, its waters enriched and modified by the tributaries that gradually flow towards it, until it at last loses itself in the ocean: so Judaism, taking its rise among the mountains of Sinai, slowly and steadily has advanced; passing alternately through a golden age of toleration and an iron age of persecution, giving its moral code for the foundation of many a government; modified by the customs and modes of life of each nation through which it has passed, chastened and enriched by centuries of experience—shall I say, as I said with the river, that it, too, at last loses itself in the great sea of humanity? No! rather like the Gulf Stream, which, passing through the vast Atlantic Ocean, part of it, and yet distinct from it, never losing its individuality, but always detected by its deeper colour and warmer temperature, until it eventually modifies the severe climate of a distant country: so Judaism, passing through all the nations of the old world, part of them, and yet distinct from them, ever recognized by its depth and intensity, has at last reached this new world without having lost its individuality. And here it is still able, by the loftiness of its ethical truth and by the purity of its principles, to give intellectual and moral stamina to a never-ending future humanity.

    M. H. HARRIS, 1887.

II

WE, more than any other nation on the globe, recall the happy day when the light of promise first dawned in a modern Canaan, overflowing with the milk and honey of humane kindness, in a land symbolized by the torch of the goddess of liberty, whose soft, mild, yet penetrating rays are reflected o'er all the scattered sons of much-tried Israel, whom she so benignantly beckons to these shores.

    ALEXANDER KOHUT, *on the 400th Anniversary of the Discovery of America*, 1892.

THE DELUGE OF FIRE

MANKIND craves the conviction that the agony and tears and suffering of these hundreds of millions of belligerents, constituting the vast majority of the human race, are not in vain; that somehow good will come of all this infinite woe.

In old Jewish books there is a wondrous legend of a second Deluge, a Deluge of Fire, that would sweep over the earth. In anticipation of it, the children of men were bidden to write the story of man on tables of clay, as such tables would not only escape destruction, but would become the more enduring. We to-day are the eyewitnesses of such a fire-deluge dreamt of by the ancients. Let us not, however, fear that civilization and religion will perish from the earth. Quite other will be its far-reaching results for mankind. Right and humanity will emerge stronger than ever from this world-conflagration. Before this war we saw that the laws of God and man were written as it were on mere tables of clay, breakable and effaceable at will. This very world-conflagration, however, will yet render the Law of Nations indestructible and for ever unassailable by insolence or power. The behests of humanity, which so far have been but pious wishes, will be converted into regulative principles in international dealings.

J. H. HERTZ, *to a congregation of Jewish soldiers at the Front, France*, 1915.

THE HEALING OF THE NATIONS

T HE sun and the moon are become black,
    And the stars withdraw their shining ...
And the heavens and the earth shall shake;
But the Lord will be a refuge unto His people.
JOEL 4. 15, 16.

AND the loftiness of man shall be bowed down,
    And the haughtiness of men shall be brought low;
    And the Lord alone shall be exalted in that day.
    And the idols shall utterly pass away.
    ISAIAH 2. 17, 18.

AND, behold, the Lord passed by, and a great and strong wind rent the
mountains, and broke in pieces the rocks before the Lord; but the Lord
was not in the wind; and after the wind an earthquake; but the Lord
was not in the earthquake; and after the earthquake a fire; but the Lord
was not in the fire; and after the fire a still small voice.
    1 KINGS 19. 11, 12.

. . .

HEAL us, O Lord, and we shall be healed; save us, and we shall be saved; for Thou art our praise. Vouchsafe a perfect healing unto all our wounds; for Thou, almighty King, art a faithful and merciful Physician.
DAILY PRAYER BOOK.

THE MESSIANIC HOPE

W HEN the harp of Judah sounded, thrilled with the touch of inspiration Divine, among the echoes it waked in the human heart were those sweet sounds whose witcheries transport the soul into the realms of happiness. That melody has been our source of courage, our solace and our strength, and in all our wanderings we have sung it. It is the music of the Messianic age, the triumph-hymn to be one day thundered by all humanity, the real psalm of life as mankind shall sing it when Israel's world-task of teaching it shall have been accomplished. Its harmony is the harmony of the families of the earth, at last at peace, at last united in brotherhood, at last happy in their return to the One Great Father.

H. PEREIRA MENDES, 1887.

HAVE we not all one father?
    Hath not one God created us?
    Why do we deal treacherously every man against his brother,
    Profaning the covenant of our fathers?
    MALACHI 2. 10.

THE VISION OF A UNITED HUMANITY

A ND it shall come to pass in the end of days,
    That the mountain of the Lord's house shall be established as
the top of the mountains,
    And shall be exalted above the hills;
    And all nations shall flow unto it,
    And many peoples shall go and say:
    'Come ye, and let us go up to the mountain of the Lord,
    To the house of the God of Jacob;
    And He will teach us of His ways;
    And we will walk in His paths.'
    For out of Zion shall go forth the law,
    And the word of the Lord from Jerusalem.
    And He shall judge between the nations,
    And shall decide for many peoples;
    And they shall beat their swords into ploughshares,
    And their spears into pruning-hooks;
    Nation shall not lift up sword against nation,
    Neither shall they learn war any more.
    ISAIAH 2. 2-4.

THE Jew who is true to himself will labour with especial energy in the cause of peace. His religion, his history, his mission, all pledge him to a policy of peace, as a citizen as well as an individual. The war-loving Jew is a contradiction in terms. The 'Man of Sorrows' must beware of helping, however remotely, to heap sorrow upon others.

MORRIS JOSEPH, 1903.

TRUST YE IN THE LORD
FOR EVER

THOU wilt keep him in perfect peace whose mind is stayed on Thee; because he trusted in Thee.

Trust ye in the Lord for ever, for the Lord is God, an everlasting Rock.

The way of the just is straight: Thou, Most Upright, makest plain the path of the just.

Yea, in the way of Thy judgements, O Lord, have we waited for Thee; to Thy name and to Thy memorial is the desire of our soul.

With my soul have I desired Thee in the night;

Yea, with my spirit within me will I seek Thee early: for when Thy judgements are in the earth, the inhabitants of the world learn righteousness.

Let favour be showed to the wicked, yet will he not learn righteousness: in the land of uprightness will he deal wrongfully and will not behold the majesty of the Lord.

Lord, Thy hand is lifted up, yet they see not: but they shall see Thy zeal for the people, and be ashamed; yea, the fire of Thine adversaries shall devour them.

Lord, Thou wilt ordain peace for us: for Thou hast also wrought all our works for us.

ISAIAH 26. 3, 4, 7-12.

PARTIE II

THE PEOPLE OF
THE BOOK

NOW the Lord said unto Abram: '... I will make of thee a great nation, and I will bless thee, and make thy name great; and be thou a blessing: And I will bless them that bless thee, and him that curseth thee will I curse; and in thee shall all the families of the earth be blessed.'

GENESIS 12. 1-3.

THUS saith God the Lord ... I the Lord have called thee in righteousness and have taken hold of thine hand, and kept thee, and set thee for a covenant of the people, for a light of the nations; to open the blind eyes, to bring out the prisoners from the dungeon, and them that sit in darkness out of the prison house.

ISAIAH 42. 5-7.

ISRAEL IMMORTAL

T HUS saith the Lord, Who giveth the sun for a light by day, and the ordinances of the moon and of the stars for a light by night, Who stirreth up the sea, that the waves thereof roar; the Lord of hosts is His name: If these ordinances depart from before Me, saith the Lord, then the seed of Israel also shall cease from being a nation before Me for ever.

JEREMIAH 31. 35, 36.

THE sun and moon for ever shine—by day
    And night they mark the Eternal's high design.
    Changeless and tireless, speeding on their way,
    The sun and moon for ever shine.
    Symbols are they of Israel's chosen line,
    A nation still, though countless foes combine;
    Smitten by God and healed by God are they:
    They shall not fear, safe 'neath the Rock divine,
    Nor cease to be, until men cease to say,
    The sun and moon for ever shine.
    YEHUDAH HALEVI, 1150. (*Trans. Alice Lucas.*)

THE life of man is numbered by days,
The days of Israel are innumerable.
ECCLESIASTICUS 37. 25.

KINGDOMS arise and kingdoms pass away, but Israel endureth for evermore.
MIDRASH.

THE ETERNAL RIDDLE

1

ISRAEL, my people,
God's greatest riddle,
Will thy solution
Ever be told?
Fought—never conquered,
Bent—never broken,
Mortal—immortal,
Youthful, though old.
Egypt enslaved thee,
Babylon crushed thee,
Rome led thee captive,
Homeless thy head.
Where are those nations
Mighty and fearsome?
Thou hast survived them,
They are long dead.
Nations keep coming,
Nations keep going,
Passing like shadows,
Wiped off the earth.
Thou an eternal

Witness remainest,
Watching their burial,
Watching their birth.
Pray, who revealed thee
Heavens great secret:
Death and destruction
Thus to defy?
Suffering torture,
Stake, inquisition—
Prithee, who taught thee
Never to die?
Ay, and who gave thee
Faith, deep as ocean,
Strong as the rock-hills,
Fierce as the sun?
Hated and hunted,
Ever thou wand'rest,
Bearing a message:
God is but one!
Pray, has thy saga
Likewise an ending,
As its beginning
Glorious of old?
Israel, my people,
God's greatest riddle,
Will thy solution
Ever be told?
P. M. RASKIN, 1914.

---

1. From *Songs of a Wanderer* (Philadelphia: Jewish Publication Society).

THE SECRET OF
ISRAEL'S IMMORTALITY

W HAT has prevented this constantly migrating people, this veritable Wandering Jew, from degenerating into brutalized vagabonds, into vagrant hordes of gipsies? The answer is at hand. In its journey through the desert of life, for eighteen centuries, the Jewish people carried along the Ark of the Covenant, which breathed into its heart ideal aspirations, and even illumined the badge of disgrace affixed to its garment with an apostolic glory. The proscribed, outlawed, universally persecuted Jew felt a sublime, noble pride in being singled out to perpetuate and to suffer for a religion which reflects eternity, by which the nations of the earth were gradually educated to a knowledge of God and morality, and from which is to spring the salvation and redemption of the world.

Such a people, which disdains its present but has the eye steadily fixed on its future, which lives as it were on hope, is on that very account eternal, like hope.

H. GRAETZ, 1853.

THE BOOK OF BOOKS

THE Bible, what a book! Large and wide as the world, based on the abysses of creation, and towering aloft into the blue secrets of heaven. Sunrise and sunset, promise and fulfilment, birth and death —the whole drama of humanity—are contained in this one book. It is the Book of Books. The Jews may readily be consoled at the loss of Jerusalem, and the Temple, and the Ark of the Covenant, and all the crown jewels of King Solomon. Such forfeiture is as naught when weighed against the Bible, the imperishable treasure that they have saved. If I do not err, it was Mahomet who named the Jews the 'People of the Book', a name which in Eastern countries has remained theirs to the present day, and is deeply significant. That one book is to the Jews their country. Within the well-fenced boundaries of that book they live and have their being; they enjoy their inalienable citizenship, are strong to admiration; thence none can dislodge them. Absorbed in the perusal of their sacred book they little heeded the changes that were wrought in the real world around them. Nations rose and vanished, States flourished and decayed, revolutions raged throughout the earth—but they, the Jews, sat poring over this book, unconscious of the wild chase of time that rushed on above their heads.

H. HEINE, 1830.

THE BIBLE

A S to an ancient temple
     Whose vast proportions tower
With summit inaccessible
Among the stars of heaven;
While the resistless ocean
Of peoples and of cities
Breaks at its feet in foam,
Work that a hundred ages
Hallow: I bow to thee.
From out thy mighty bosom
Rise hymns sublime, and melodies
Like to the heavens singing
Praises to their Creator;
While at the sound, an ecstasy,
A trance, fills all my being
With terror and with awe—
I feel my proud heart thrilling
With throbs of holy pride.
Oh! come, thou high beneficent
Heritage of my fathers;
Our country, altar, prophet,
Our life, our all, art thou!

In doubt, in woe, in outrage,
In pangs of dissolution
That wring our tortured hearts,
Come, ope the rosy portals
Of Hope to us once more.
Ah me! what countless miseries,
What tears all unregarded.
Hast thou consoled and softened
With gentle voice and holy!
How many hearts that struggle
With doubt, remorse, anxiety,
With all the woes of ages,
Dost thou, on ample pinions,
Lift purified to Heaven!
Listen! the world is rising,
Seeking, unquiet, thrilling,
Awakens the new century
To new hopes and new visions.
Men hear upon the mountains
Strange and life-giving voices;
Every soul seems to wait,
And from that Book the signal
For the new day shall come.
DAVID LEVI, 1846. (*Trans. Mary A. Craig.*)

FROM century to century, even unto this day, through the fairest regions of civilization, the Bible dominates existence. Its vision of life moulds states and societies. Its Psalms are more popular in every country than the poems of the nation's own poets. Beside this one book with its infinite editions ... all other literatures seem 'trifles light as air'.
ISRAEL ZANGWILL, 1895.

A JEWISH VERSION OF
THE BIBLE

I

OUR great claim to the gratitude of mankind is that we gave to the world the word of God, the Bible. We have stormed heaven to snatch down this heavenly gift, as the Paitan[1] puts it. We threw ourselves into the breach, and covered it with our bodies against every attack. We allowed ourselves to be slain in hundreds and thousands rather than become unfaithful to it, and we bore witness to its truth, and watched over its purity, in the face of a hostile world. The Bible is our sole *raison d'être*; and it is just this which the Higher Anti-Semitism, both within and without our ranks, is seeking to destroy, denying all our claims for the past and leaving us without hope for the future. This intellectual persecution can only be fought with intellectual weapons, and unless we make an effort to recover our Bible we are irrevocably lost from both worlds.

S. SCHECHTER, 1903.

II

THERE is an old tradition that the day on which, for the first time, the Pentateuch was translated into a foreign language—into Greek—was considered by Jews as a day of great national calamity. It was feared that the translation, being incorrect, might become the source of error instead of being the fountain of divine truths. The fear felt and expressed about two thousand years ago has been fully justified by the history of the several versions that have since been undertaken, and by the large number of false doctrines, supposed to be founded on the authority of Holy Writ, whilst really originating in mistakes made by translators.

    M. FRIEDLÄNDER, 1886.

NEW translations of the Bible have appeared and are appearing in various languages; but none of them has made, or intends to make, a complete and exhaustive use of Jewish contributions to the subject. Great university professors who know much, very much, but who do not know Jewish literature, unconsciously assume that they do not know it because it is not worth knowing—a judgement that no man has a right to pronounce until he has studied it—and this they have not done.

    M. SULZBERGER, 1898.

THE book, commonly known as the Authorized, or King James's Version, has been so long looked upon with a deep veneration almost bordering on superstitious dread, that, to most persons, the very thought of furnishing an improved translation of the Divine records will be viewed as an impious assumption and a contempt of the wisdom of former ages. Since the time of King James, however, the world has progressed in biblical knowledge no less than in all other branches of science; and giant minds have laboured to make clear what formerly was obscure.

    ISAAC LEESER, 1855.

I FULLY admit the great merits of the Revised Version of the Bible. It corrects many faults, amends many mistranslations of the so-called King James's Version, without impairing the antique charm of the English Bible, without putting out of tune the music so dear to our ears. Yet even that great work, compiled by the most eminent scholars and learned theologians in the land, is disfigured by errors due to dogmatic preconceptions.

HERMANN ADLER, 1896.

III

THE present translation[2] has a character of its own. It aims to combine the spirit of Jewish tradition with the results of biblical scholarship, ancient, mediaeval, and modern. It gives to the Jewish world a translation of the Scriptures done by men imbued with the Jewish consciousness, while the non-Jewish world, it is hoped, will welcome a translation that presents many passages from the Jewish traditional point of view.

The Jew cannot afford to have his own Bible translation prepared for him by others. He cannot have it as a gift, even as he cannot borrow his soul from others. If a new country and a new language metamorphose him into a new man, the duty of this new man is to prepare a new garb and a new method of expression for what is most sacred and most dear to him.

From TRANSLATORS' PREFACE, *Jewish Version of the Bible, 1916.*

IV

SCRIPTURE must be interpreted according to its plain, natural sense, each word according to the context. Traditional exposition, however, may also be taken to heart, as it is said: 'Is not My word like as fire?'—consisting of many sparks—'and like a hammer that breaketh the rock in pieces?'—and therefore capable of various explanations.

RASHI, 1080.

V

THERE is none that hath ever made an end of learning it, and there is none that will ever find out all its mysteries. For its wisdom is richer than any sea, and its word deeper than any abyss.

ECCLESIASTICUS 24. 28, 29.

1. Name for Synagogue liturgical poet.
2. The Holy Scriptures: A New Translation, with the aid of previous versions and with constant consultation of Jewish Authorities. Jewish Publication Society, Philadelphia.

ISRAEL THE PEOPLE OF
REVELATION

H AD there been no Israelites there would be no Torah. Israel's
pre-eminence is not derived from Moses, it is Moses whose pre-
eminence is due to Israel. The Divine love went out towards the multitude of the children of the Patriarchs, the Congregation of Jacob.
Moses was merely the divinely chosen instrument through whom
God's Blessing was to be assured unto them. We are called not the
people of Moses, but the people of God.

YEHUDAH HALEVI, 1141.

THE Greeks were not all artists, but the Greek nation was alone
capable of producing a Phidias or a Praxiteles. The same was the case
with Judaism. It is certain that not all Jews were prophets; the exclama-
tion, 'Would that all the people of the Lord were prophets!' was a pious
wish. Nevertheless, Israel is the people of Revelation. It must have had
a native endowment that could produce, that could rear, such men. Nor
does Judaism claim to be the work of single individuals; it does not
speak of the God of Moses, nor of the God of the Prophets, but of the
God of Israel. The fact that the greatest prophet left his work unfinished contains a profound truth. *No man knoweth of his sepulchre unto
this day.* Thereon our ancient teachers remark: 'His grave should not

serve as a place of pilgrimage whither men go to do honour to *one man*, and thus raise him above the level of man'.

A. GEIGER, 1865.

THERE IS NO GOD BUT
GOD AND ISRAEL IS
HIS PROPHET

1

WHEN one thinks how this earliest of theistic creeds has persisted through the ages, by what wonderful constructive statecraft it has built up a race of which the lowest unit is no atom in a 'submerged tenth', but an equal member of a great historic brotherhood, a scion of the oldest of surviving civilizations, a student of sacred books, a lover of home and peace; when one remembers how he has agonized—the great misunderstood of history—how his 'pestilent heresy' has been chastised and rebuked by Popes and Crusaders, Inquisitors and Missionaries, how he has remained sublimely protestant, imperturbable amid marvellous cathedrals and all the splendid shows of Christendom, and how despite all and after all he is living to see the world turning slowly back to his vision of life; then one seems to see the 'finger of God', the hand of the Master-Artist, behind the comedy-tragedy of existence, to believe that Israel is veritably a nation with a mission, that there is no God but God and Israel is His prophet.

ISRAEL ZANGWILL.

1. From 'The Position of Judaism', *North American Review*, April, 1895.

MOSES

HOW small Sinai appears when Moses stands upon it! This mountain is only the pedestal for the feet of the man whose head reaches up to the heavens, where he speaks with God.... Formerly I could not pardon the legislator of the Jews his hatred against the plastic arts. I did not see that, notwithstanding his hostility to art, Moses was a great artist, and possessed the true artistic spirit. But this spirit was directed by him, as by his Egyptian compatriots, to colossal and indestructible undertakings. He built human pyramids, carved human obelisks; he took a poor shepherd family and created a nation from it—a great, eternal, holy people; a people of God, destined to outlive the centuries, and to serve as a pattern to all other nations, even as a prototype to the whole of mankind. He created Israel.

As of the master-builder, so of his work—the Hebrew people—I did not speak with sufficient reverence. I see now that the Greeks were only handsome youths, whilst the Jews were always men—powerful, indomitable men—who have fought and suffered on every battlefield of human thought.

H. HEINE, 1854.

THE PROPHETS

I

'TIS a little people, but it has done great things. It had but a precarious hold on a few crags and highlands between the desert and the deep sea, yet its thinkers and sages with eagle vision took into their thought the destinies of all humanity, and rang out in clarion voice a message of hope to the downtrodden of all races. Claiming for themselves and their people the duty and obligations of a true aristocracy, they held forth to the peoples ideals of a true democracy founded on right and justice. Their voices have never ceased to re-echo around the world, and the greatest things that have been done to raise men's lot have been always in the spirit, often in the name, of the Hebrew prophets.

JOSEPH JACOBS, 1919.

THE mere foretelling of future events is the lowest stage of prophecy, and in the eyes of the great Prophets of Israel it was of quite secondary importance. Their aim was to fathom the secrets of holiness; and their striving, by means of admonition and moral suasion, to guide the peoples in the paths which lead mankind to spiritual and political well-being.

SHEMTOB IBN SHEMTOB, 1489.

II

IT was part of the spirit of Prophecy to be dumb-founded at human ferocity as at something against nature and reason. In the presence of the iniquities of the world, the heart of the Prophets bled as though from a wound of the Divine Spirit, and their cry of indignation re-echoed the wrath of the Deity. Greece and Rome had their rich and poor, just as Israel had in the days of Jeroboam II, and the various classes continued to slaughter one another for centuries; but no voice of justice and pity arose from the fierce tumult. Therefore the words of the Prophets have more vitality at the present time, and answer better to the needs of modern souls, than all the classic masterpieces of antiquity.

JAMES DARMESTETER, 1891.

IN Hebrew prophecy we have no crumbling monument of perishable stone, the silent witness of a past that is dead and gone, but the quicke-ning breath of the spirit itself. In the ardent souls of the Prophets the thought of Deity was centred as in a burning-glass—a fire that consumed them, a shining light for men. Theirs was the abiding sense of an eternal Will and Purpose underlying human transient schemes, an eternal Presence, transfusing all of life as with a hidden flame; so that love of country, love of right, love of man, were not alone human things, but also divine, because they were embraced and focussed in a single living unity—the love of God.

JOSEPHINE LAZARUS, 1893.

THE TALMUD

T HE Talmud is the work which embodies the civil and canonical law of the Jewish people, forming a kind of supplement to the Pentateuch—a supplement such as took 1,000 years of a nation's life to produce. It is not merely a dull treatise, but it appeals to the imagination and the feelings, and to all that is noblest and purest. Between the rugged boulders of the law which bestrew the path of the Talmud there grow the blue flowers of romance—parable, tale, gnome, saga; its elements are taken from heaven and earth, but chiefly and most lovingly from the human heart and from Scripture, for every verse and every word in this latter became, as it were, a golden nail upon which it hung its gorgeous tapestries.

The fundamental law of all human and social economy in the Talmud was the absolute equality of men. It was pointed out that man was created alone—lest one should say to another, 'I am of the better or earlier stock'. In a discussion that arose among the Masters as to which was the most important passage in the whole Bible, one pointed to the verse 'And thou shalt love thy neighbour as thyself'. The other contradicted him and pointed to the words 'This is the book of the generations of man' (Gen. 5. 1)—not black, not white, not great, not small, but *man*.

'The law given on Mount Sinai', the Masters said, 'though emphatically addressed to one people, belongs to all humanity. It was not given in any king's land, not in any city or inhabited spot—it was given on God's own highway, in the desert—not in the darkness and stillness of night, but in plain day, amid thunder and lightning. And why was it given on Sinai? Because it is the lowliest of mountains—to show that God's spirit rests only upon them that are meek and lowly in their hearts.'

The Talmud taught that religion was not a thing of creed or dogma or faith merely, but of active goodness. Scripture said, 'Ye shall walk in the ways of the Lord'. 'But the Lord is a consuming fire; how can men walk in His ways?' 'By being', the rabbis answered, 'as He is—merciful, loving, long-suffering. Mark how on the first page of the Pentateuch God clothed the naked—Adam; and on the last he buried the dead—Moses. He heals the sick, frees the captives, does good to His enemies, and is merciful both to the living and to the dead.'

The most transcendental love of the rabbis was lavished on children. All the verses of Scripture that spoke of flowers and gardens were applied to children and schools. The highest and most exalted title which they bestowed in their poetical flights upon God Himself was that of 'Pedagogue of Man'. Indeed, the relationship of man to God they could not express more pregnantly than by the most familiar words which occur from one end of the Talmud to the other, 'Our Father in Heaven'.

I have been able to bring before you what proves, as it were, but a drop in the vast ocean of Talmud—that strange, wild, weird ocean, with its leviathans, and its wrecks of golden argosies, and with its forlorn bells that send up their dreamy sounds ever and anon, while the fisherman bends upon his oar, and starts and listens, and perchance the tears may come into his eyes.

EMANUEL DEUTSCH, 1868.

JEWISH LITERATURE

R ABBINISM was a sequel to the Bible, and if, like all sequels, it was unequal to its original, it nevertheless shared its greatness. The works of all Jews up to the modern period were the sequel to this sequel. Through them all may be detected the unifying principle that literature in its truest sense includes life itself; that intellect is the hand-maid to conscience; and that the best books are those which best teach men how to live. This underlying unity gave more harmony to Jewish literature than is possessed by many literatures more distinctively national. The maxim 'Righteousness delivers from death' applies to books as well as to men. A literature whose consistent theme is Righteousness, is immortal.

I. ABRAHAMS, 1899.

THE WORK OF THE RABBIS

JUDAISM and the Bible are by no means identical; the Bible is only one constituent part of Judaism, though the most fundamental one. Who taught the average Jew to understand his Judaism, to love his religion and his God? Without the zeal of the Rabbis, the Bible would never have become the guide of every Jew. They translated it into the vernacular for the people, and expounded it to the masses. They taught them not to despair under the tortures of the present, but to look forward to the future. At the same time they developed the spirit of the Bible and never lost sight of the lofty teachings of the Prophets. It is the immortal merit of the unknown Rabbis of the centuries immediately before and after the common era that they found and applied the proper 'fences' for the preservation of Judaism, and that they succeeded in rescuing real morality and pure monotheism for the ages that were to follow.

A. BÜCHLER, 1908.

ISRAEL'S HISTORY NEVER-
ENDING

I SRAEL'S 'Heroic History', as Manasseh ben Israel called it, is in
truth never-ending. Line upon line is still being added,
and *finis* will never be written on the page of Jewish history till the
Light which shineth more and more unto the Perfect Day shall fall
upon it, and illumine the whole beautiful world. Each Jew and each
Jewess is making his or her mark, or his or her stain, upon the
wonderful unfinished history of the Jews, the history which Herder
called the greatest poem of all time. *'Ye are my witnesses', saith the
Lord.* Loyal and steadfast witnesses is it, or self-seeking and suborned
ones? A witness of some sort every Jew born is bound to be. He must
fulfil his mission, and through good report and through evil report, and
though it be only writ in water, he must add his item of evidence to the
record that all who run may read.
LADY MAGNUS, 1886.

THE story of this little sect—the most remarkable survival of the fittest
known to humanity—in no way corresponds with its numbers; it is not
a tale of majorities. It is a story that begins very near the beginning of
history, and shows little sign of drawing to a conclusion. It is a story
that has chapters in every country on earth, that has borne the impress

of every period. All men and all ages pass through it in unending procession.

ISRAEL ZANGWILL, 1895.

THE MEANING OF JEWISH HISTORY

M AN is made man by history. It is history that causes the men of historic nations to be more civilized than the savage. The Jew recognizes that he is made what he is by the history of his fathers, and feels he is losing his better self so far as he loses his hold on his past history.

JOSEPH JACOBS, 1889.

ISRAEL is the heart of mankind.

YEHUDAH HALEVI.

THE high-road of Jewish history leads to wide outlooks. That which is great and lasting in Jewish history is the spiritual wealth accumulated through the ages; the description of the fierce battles fought between the powers of darkness and light, of freedom and persecution, of knowledge and ignorance. Our great men are the heroes of the school and the sages of the synagogue, not the knights of the sanguinary battlefield. No widow was left to mourn through our victory, no mother for her lost son, no orphan for the lost father.

M. GASTER, 1906.

THE HALLOWING OF
JEWISH HISTORY

T HE first part of Jewish history, the Biblical part, is a source from
which, for many centuries, millions of human beings belonging
to the most diverse denominations have derived instruction, solace, and
inspiration. Its heroes have long ago become types, incarnations, of
great ideas. The events it relates serve as living ethical formulas. But a
time will come—perhaps it is not very far off—when the second half
of Jewish history, the record of the two thousand years of the Jewish
people's life after the Biblical period, will be accorded the same treat-
ment. The thousand years' martyrdom of the Jewish people, its
unbroken pilgrimage, its tragic fate, its teachers of religion, its martyrs,
philosophers, champions—this whole epic will in days to come sink
deep into the memory of men. It will speak to the heart and conscience
of men, not merely to their curious mind. It will secure respect for the
silvery hair of the Jewish people, a people of thinkers and sufferers. It
is our firm conviction that the time is approaching in which the second
half of Jewish history will be to the noblest part of *thinking* humanity
what its first half has long been to *believing* humanity, a source of
sublime moral truths.

S. M. DUBNOW, 1893.

ISRAEL'S MARTYRDOM

I F there are ranks in suffering, Israel takes precedence of all the nations; if the duration of sorrows and the patience with which they are borne ennoble, the Jews can challenge the aristocracy of every land; if a literature is called rich in the possession of a few classic tragedies—what shall we say to a National Tragedy lasting for fifteen hundred years, in which the poets and the actors were also the heroes?
LEOPOLD ZUNZ, 1855.

COMBINE all the woes that temporal and ecclesiastical tyrannies have ever inflicted on men or nations, and you will not have reached the full measure of suffering which this martyr people was called upon to endure century upon century. It was as if all the powers of earth had conspired—and they did so conspire—to exterminate the Jewish people, or at least to transform it into a brutalized horde. History dare not pass over in silence these scenes of wellnigh unutterable misery. It is her duty to give a true and vivid account of them; to evoke due admiration for the superhuman endurance of this suffering people, and to testify that Israel, like his ancestor in the days of old, has striven with gods and with men, and has prevailed.
H. GRAETZ.

UNDER THE ROMAN
EMPERORS

THERE had now a tumult arisen in Alexandria between the Jewish inhabitants and the Greeks, and three ambassadors were chosen out of each party that were at variance who came to Caius (Caligula). Now, one of the Greek ambassadors was Apion, who uttered many blasphemies against the Jews; and among other things he said that while all who were subject to the Roman Empire built altars and temples to Caesar, and in other regards universally received him as they received the gods, these Jews alone thought it a dishonourable thing for them to erect statues in honour of him, as well as to swear by his name.

Hereupon Caligula, taking it very heinously that he should be thus despised by the Jews alone, gave orders to make an invasion of Judea with a great body of troops, and, if they were obstinate, to conquer them by war, and then to erect the statues. Accordingly Petronius, the Governor of Syria, got together as great a number of auxiliaries as he possibly could, and took with him two legions of the Roman army. But there came many ten thousands of the Jews to Petronius, to offer their petitions to him, that he would not compel them to transgress and violate the law of their forefathers. 'If', said they, 'thou art entirely resolved to bring this statue, and erect it, do thou first kill us, and then do what thou hast resolved on; for, while we are alive, we cannot permit such things as are forbidden us to be done by the authority of our Legislator.'

Petronius then hasted to Tiberias; and many thousands of the Jews met Petronius again, when he was come to Tiberias. Then Petronius said to them: 'Will you then make war with Caesar without considering his great preparations for war and your own weakness?' They replied: 'We will not by any means make war with him, but still we will die before we see our laws transgressed'. So they threw themselves down upon their faces, and stretched out their throats, and said they were ready to be slain. Thus they continued in their resolution, and proposed to themselves to die willingly rather than to see the dedication of the statue[1].

FLAVIUS JOSEPHUS, 1st cent.

IN the world-wide Roman Empire it was the Jews alone who refused the erection of statues and the paying of divine honours to Caligula, and *thereby saved the honour of the human race* when all the other peoples slavishly obeyed the decree of the Imperial madman.

J. FUERST, 1890.

---

1. Only the sudden death of the deranged emperor saved the defenceless population from fearful massacre.

IN MEDIAEVAL ROME

I N the whole history of heroism there is nothing finer than the
example of the Jews of the Roman Ghetto, a handful of men who
for 1,500 years and longer remained true to their own ideals—
unmoved and undazzled by the triumphant world-power of the dominant faith; and undaunted

By the torture prolonged from age to age,
By the infamy, Israel's heritage,
By the Ghetto's plague, by the garb's disgrace,
By the badge of shame, by the felon's place,
By the branding tool, by the bloody whip,
And the summons to Christian fellowship.

Helpless victims of all the horrors enumerated in these burning
lines of Robert Browning, these Jews were yet *free men*. Not a trace of
what a modern Jewish thinker—Achad Ha'am—has called 'spiritual
slavery' was theirs. In all fundamental matters they were totally indif-
ferent to the opinion of those who might torture the body but could
never crush the soul.

J. H. HERTZ, 1915.

THE history of the daughter religions of Judaism is one uninterrupted
series of attempts to commit matricide.

M. STEINSCHNEIDER, 1893.

THE FIRST CRUSADE (1096)

1

YEA, they slay us and they smite,
Vex our souls with sore affright;
All the closer cleave we, Lord,
To Thine everlasting word.
Not a word of all their Mass
Shall our lips in homage pass;
Though they curse, and bind, and kill,
The living God is with us still.
We still are Thine, though limbs are torn;
Better death than life forsworn.
Noblest matrons seek for death,
Rob their children of their breath;
Fathers, in their fiery zeal,
Slay their sons with murderous steel,
And in heat of holiest strife,
For love of Thee, spare not their life.
The fair and young lie down to die
In witness of Thy Unity;
From dying lips the accents swell,
'Thy God is One, O Israel';
And bridegroom answers unto bride,

'The Lord is God, and none beside',
And, knit with bonds of holiest faith,
They pass to endless life through death.
KALONYMOS BEN YEHUDAH. (*Trans. E. H. Plumptre.*)

---

1. The Jewish communities in the Rhine region were then decimated by massacre or by self-immolation in order to escape baptism.

THE SECOND CRUSADE

IN the year 1146 Israel's communities were terror-stricken. The
monk Rudolph who shamefully persecuted Israel, arose against the
people of God, in order, like Haman of old, to destroy, to slay, and to
cause to perish. He travelled throughout Germany to bestow the cross
of the crusaders upon all who consented to set out for Jerusalem to
fight against the Moslems. In every place where he came he aroused
the people, crying, 'Avenge ye first the vengeance of our God on His
enemies who are here before us, and then we will go forward'. When
the Jews heard this, their courage failed them by reason of the rage of
their oppressor who sought their destruction. They cried to God,
saying: 'Alas, O Lord God! Behold fifty years, like the period of a
jubilee, have not yet elapsed since we shed our blood like water to
sanctify Thy holy, great, and revered Name, on the day of the great
slaughter. Wilt Thou indeed forsake us for ever and extend Thy wrath
against us unto all generations? Shall misery follow misery?'

The Lord heard our supplications, and turned unto us, and had pity
upon us, according to His abundant loving-kindness. He sent one of
their greatest and respected teachers, the abbot Bernard, from the town
Clairvaux in France, after this evil monk. And he also preached to his
people according to their custom, crying 'It is good that you are ready
to go forth against the Moslems; but whosoever uses violence against
the Jews commits a deadly sin'.

All honoured this monk as one of their saints, neither has it ever been said that he received a bribe for his good service to us. Many desisted from any further murderous attacks against us. We gladly gave our possessions as a ransom for our lives. Whatever was asked of us, silver or gold, we withheld not.

If our Creator in His great compassion had not sent us this abbot, there would have been none in Israel that would have escaped or remained alive. Blessed be He who saves and delivers. Praised be His Name.

EPHRAIM OF BONN, 1180.

JEWISH SUFFERING

B REAK forth in lamentation,
My agonizing song,
That like a lava-torrent
Has boiled within me long.
My song shall thrill each hearer,
And none so deaf but hears,
For the burden of my ditty
Is the pain of a thousand years.
It melts both gentle and simple,
Even hearts of stone are riven—
Sets women and flowers weeping;
They weep, the stars of heaven.
And all these tears are flowing
By channels still and wide,
Homeward they are all flowing
To meet in Jordan's tide.
H. HEINE, 1824.

THE JEWS OF YORK (1190)

W HEN Richard I ascended the throne, the Jews, to conciliate the Royal protection, brought their tributes. Many had hastened from remote parts of England, and, appearing at Westminster, the Court and the mob imagined that they had leagued to bewitch His Majesty. A rumour spread rapidly through the city that in honour of the festival the Jews were to be massacred. The populace, at once eager of Royalty and riot, pillaged and burnt their houses and murdered the devoted Jews.

The people of York soon gathered to imitate the people of London. The alarmed Jews hastened to Jocenus, the most opulent of the Jews, who conducted them to the Governor of York Castle, and prevailed on him to afford them an asylum for their persons and effects.

The castle had sufficient strength for their defence; but a suspicion arising that the Governor, who often went out, intended to betray them, they one day refused him entrance. He complained to the sheriff of the county; and the chiefs of the violent party, who stood deeply indebted to the Jews, uniting with him, orders were issued to attack the castle. The cruel multitude, united with the soldiery, felt such a desire of slaughtering those they intended to despoil, that the sheriff, repenting of the order, revoked it; but in vain: fanaticism and robbery once set loose will satiate their appetency for blood and plunder. The attacks continued, till at length the Jews perceived they could hold out no longer, and a council was called to consider what remained to be done in the extremity of danger.

When the Jewish council was assembled, the Haham[1] rose, and addressed them in this manner: 'Men of Israel! the God of our ancestors is omniscient, and there is no one who can say, Why doest Thou this? This day He commands us to die for His Law; for that Law which we have cherished from the first hour it was given, which we have preserved pure throughout our captivity in all nations; and for which, because of the many consolations it has given us and the eternal hope it communicates, can we do less than die? Death is before our eyes; and we have only to choose an honourable and easy one. If we fall into the hands of our enemies, which you know we cannot escape, our death will be ignominious and cruel. It is therefore my advice that we elude their tortures; that we ourselves should be our own executioners; and that we voluntarily surrender our lives to our Creator. God seems to call for us, but let us not be unworthy of that call.' Having said this, the old man sat down and wept.

The assembly was divided in its opinions. Again the Rabbin rose, and spoke these few words in a firm and decisive tone. 'My children! since we are not unanimous in our opinions, let those who do not approve of my advice depart from this assembly!' Some departed, but the greater number attached themselves to their venerable priest. They now employed themselves in consuming their valuables by fire; and every man, fearful of trusting to the timid and irresolute hand of the women, first destroyed his wife and children, and then himself. Jocenus and the Rabbin alone remained. Their life was protracted to the last, that they might see everything performed according to their orders. Jocenus, being the chief Jew, was distinguished by the last mark of human respect in receiving his death from the consecrated hand of the aged Rabbin, who immediately after performed the melancholy duty on himself.

All this was transacted in the depth of the night. In the morning the walls of the castle were seen wrapt in flames, and only a few miserable and pusillanimous beings, unworthy of the sword, were viewed on the battlements pointing to their extinct brethren. When they opened the gates of the castle, these men verified the prediction of their late Rabbin; for the multitude, bursting through the solitary courts, found themselves defrauded of their hopes, and in a moment avenged themselves on the feeble wretches who knew not to die with honour.

ISAAC D'ISRAELI, 1793.

---

1. Term for 'rabbi' among Sephardi Jews.

THE EXPULSION FROM SPAIN, 1492

L OOK, they move! No comrades near but curses;
　　 Tears gleam in beards of men sore with reverses;
Flowers from fields abandoned, loving nurses,
Fondly deck the women's raven hair.
Faded, scentless flowers that shall remind them
Of their precious homes and graves behind them;
Old men, clasping Torah-scrolls, unbind them,
Lift the parchment flags and silent lead.
Mock not with thy light, O sun, our morrow;
Cease not, cease not, O ye songs of sorrow;
From what land a refuge can we borrow,
Weary, thrust out, God-forsaken we?
Could ye, suff'ring souls, peer through the Future,
From despair ye would awake to rapture;
Lo! The Genoese boldly steers to capture
Freedom's realm beyond an unsailed sea![1]
L. A. FRANKL. (*Trans. by M. D. Louis.*)

---

1. On the day following the expulsion, Columbus set sail for the discovery of America.

THE EXODUS (AUGUST 3, 1492)

T HE Spanish noon is a blaze of azure fire, and the dusty pilgrims crawl like an endless serpent along treeless plains and bleached high-roads, through rock-split ravines and castellated, cathedral-shadowed towns.

2. The hoary patriarch, wrinkled as an almond shell, bows painfully upon his staff. The beautiful young mother, ivory-pale, wellnigh swoons beneath her burden; in her large enfolding arms nestles her sleeping babe, round her knees flock her little ones with bruised and bleeding feet. 'Mother, shall we soon be there?'

3. The halt, the blind, are amid the train. Sturdy pack-horses laboriously drag the tented wagons wherein lie the sick athirst with fever.

4. The panting mules are urged forward by spur and goad; stuffed are the heavy saddle-bags with the wreckage of ruined homes.

5. Hark to the tinkling silver bells that adorn the tenderly carried silken scrolls.

6. Noble and abject, learned and simple, illustrious and obscure, plod side by side, all brothers now, all merged in one routed army of misfortune.

7. Woe to the straggler who falls by the wayside! No friend shall close his eyes.

8. They leave behind the grape, the olive, and the fig; the vines they planted, the corn they sowed, the garden-cities of Andalusia and

Aragon, Estremadura and La Mancha, of Granada and Castile; the altar, the hearth, and the grave of their fathers.

9. The townsman spits at their garments, the shepherd quits his flock, the peasant his plough, to pelt with curses and stones; the villager sets on their trail his yelping cur.

10. Oh, the weary march! oh, the uptorn roots of home! oh, the blankness of the receding goal!

11. Listen to their lamentations. *They that ate dainty food are desolate in the streets; they were reared in scarlet embrace dunghills. They flee away and wander about. Men say among the nations, They shall no more sojourn there; our end is near, our days are full, our doom is come.* (Lam. 4. 5, 15, 18.)

12. Whither shall they turn? for the West hath cast them out, and the East refuseth to receive.

EMMA LAZARUS, 1883.

A SONG OF REDEMPTION

S URELY a limit boundeth every woe,
　　But mine enduring anguish hath no end;
My grievous years are spent in ceaseless flow,
My wound hath no amend.
O'erwhelmed, my helm doth fail, no hand is strong
To steer the bark to port, her longed-for aim.
How long, O Lord, wilt Thou my doom prolong?
When shall be heard the Dove's[1] sweet voice of song?
O leave us not to perish for our wrong,
Who bear Thy Name!
Wherefore wilt Thou forget us, Lord, for aye?
Mercy we crave!
O Lord, we hope in Thee alway,
Our King will save!
Wounded and crushed beneath my load I sigh,
Despised and abject, outcast, trampled low;
How long, O Lord, shall I of violence cry,
My heart dissolve with woe?
How many years without a gleam of light
Has thraldom been our lot, our portion pain?
With Ishmael[2] as a lion in his might,
And Persia as an owl of darksome night,

Beset on either side, behold our plight
Betwixt the twain.
Wherefore wilt Thou forget us, Lord, for aye?
Mercy we crave!
O Lord, we hope in Thee alway,
Our King will save!
SOLOMON IBN GABIROL, 1050. (*Trans. Nina Salaman.*)

---

1. Poetic name for Israel.
2. 'Ishmael' and 'Persia' stand for Mohammedan and Christian Powers respectively.

SHYLOCK

S HYLOCK is 'the Jew that Shakespeare drew'. He is not the Jew of real life, even in the Middle Ages, stained as their story is with the hot tears—nay, the very heart's blood—of the martyred race. The mediaeval Jew did not take vengeance on his cruel foes. Nay, more than this: with a sublime magnanimity he could actually preach and practise widest benevolence towards his oppressors. Throughout the Middle Ages, when Jews were daily plundered and tortured, and done to death 'for the glory of God', not a word was breathed against the morality of the victims. They suffered because they were heretics, because they would not juggle with their conscience and profess a belief that did not live in their souls.

But Jewish ethics soared to still nobler heights. The Jew preserved his integrity in spite of his suffering; but more than this, he forgave—ay, even blessed—its authors. The Jews hunted out of Spain in 1492 were in turn cruelly expelled from Portugal. Some took refuge on the African coast. Eighty years later the descendants of the men who had committed or allowed these enormities were defeated in Africa, whither they had been led by their king, Dom Sebastian. Those who were not slain were offered as slaves at Fez to the descendants of the Jewish exiles from Portugal. 'The humbled Portuguese nobles', the historian narrates, 'were comforted when their purchasers proved to be Jews, for they knew that they had humane hearts.'

MORRIS JOSEPH, 1891.

ON THE EVE OF THE RE-SETTLEMENT IN ENGLAND

THE Lord, blessed for ever, by His prophet Jeremiah (chap. 29. 7) gives it in command to the captive Israelites that were dispersed among the heathens, that they should continually pray for and endeavour the peace, welfare, and prosperity of the city wherein they dwelt and the inhabitants thereof. This the Jews have always done, and continue to this day in all their synagogues, with a particular blessing of the prince or magistrate under whose protection they live. And this the Right Honourable my Lord St. John can testify, who, when he was ambassador to the Lords the States of the United Provinces, was pleased to honour our synagogue at Amsterdam with his presence, where our nation entertained him with music and all expressions of joy and gladness, and also pronounced a blessing, not only upon His Honour then present, but upon the whole Commonwealth of England, for that they were a people in league and amity, and because we conceived some hopes that they would manifest towards us what we ever bare towards them, viz. all love and affection.

MANASSEH BEN ISRAEL, 1656.

JEWISH EMANCIPATION

THE whole question of emancipation, as it concerns only our external condition, is in Judaism but of secondary interest. Sooner or later the nations will decide the question between right and wrong, between humanity and inhumanity; and the first awakening of a higher calling than the mere lust for possession and enjoyment, the first expression of a nobler recognition of God as the only Lord and Father, and of the earth as a Holy Land assigned by Him to all men for the fulfilment of their human calling—will find its expression everywhere in the emancipation of all who are oppressed, including the Jews. We have a higher object to attain, and this is entirely in our own hands— the ennobling of ourselves, the realization of Judaism by Jews.

SAMSON RAPHAEL HIRSCH, 1836. (*Trans. B. Drachmann.*)

IF the political privileges we have gained could in any way weaken our Jewish sympathies, they would have been purchased at a terrible cost, and would signally defeat the intentions of those who aided and laboured for the movement.

BARON LIONEL DE ROTHSCHILD, 1869.

THE JEWISH QUESTION

T O approach the Jewish question is to be confronted with every great question of the day—social, political, financial, humanitarian, national, and religious. Each phase should be treated by an expert; but however discussed or dealt with, there is one point of view which should never be lost sight of, namely, the point of view of humanity. First and foremost we must be human if we would raise our voice on so human a theme.

JOSEPHINE LAZARUS, 1892.

EVERY country has the Jews it deserves.

K. E. FRANZOS, 1875.

TO base the appeal for justice to present-day Jewry upon the cultural services of ancient Israel would be treason to the inalienable rights of man. A people may for a time be robbed of these rights, but—whatever the alleged political reason for such a crime—it cannot be legally or equitably deprived of them.

M. STEINSCHNEIDER, 1893.

IN a free State, it is not the Christian that rules the Jew, neither is it the Jew that rules the Christian; it is Justice that rules.
LEOPOLD ZUNZ, 1859.

THE JEWS OF ENGLAND
(1290-1902)

1

AN Edward's England spat us out—a band
Foredoomed to redden Vistula or Rhine,
And leaf-like toss with every wind malign.
All mocked the faith they could not understand.
Six centuries have passed. The yellow brand
On shoulder nor on soul has left a sign,
And on our brows must Edward's England twine
Her civic laurels with an equal hand.
Thick-clustered stars of fierce supremacy
Upon the martial breast of England glance!
She seems of War the very Deity.
Could aught remain her glory to enhance?
Yea, for I count her noblest victory
Her triumph o'er her own intolerance.
ISRAEL ZANGWILL, 1902.

1. From *Blind Children* (London: Heinemann).

WELCOME OF THE HEBREW CONGREGATION, NEWPORT,RHODE ISLAND, U.S.A., TO GEORGE WASHINGTON

1

SIR,

Permit the Children of the Stock of Abraham to approach you with the most cordial affection and esteem for your person and merits, and to join with your fellow citizens in welcoming you to Newport.

Deprived as we heretofore have been of the invaluable rights of free citizens, we now (with a deep sense of gratitude to the Almighty Disposer of all events) behold a Government erected by the Majesty of the people—a Government which to bigotry gives no sanction, to persecution no assistance, but generously affording to all, liberty of conscience, and immunities of citizenship, deeming every one, of whatever Nation, tongue, or language, equal parts of the great Government Machine. This so ample and extensive Federal Union, whose basis is Philanthropy, Mutual Confidence, and Public Virtue, we cannot but acknowledge to be the work of the great God, Who ruleth in the Armies of Heaven, and among the inhabitants of the earth, doing whatever seemeth Him good.

For all the blessings of civil and religious liberty which we enjoy under an equal and benign administration, we desire to send up our thanks to the Ancient of Days, the great Preserver of men, beseeching

Him that the Angel who conducted our forefathers through the Wilderness into the Promised Land may graciously conduct you through all the difficulties and dangers of this mortal life. And when, like Joshua, full of days and full of honour, you are gathered to your Fathers, may you be admitted into the Heavenly Paradise to partake of the water of life and the tree of immortality.

Done and signed by order of the Hebrew Congregation in Newport, Rhode Island, August 17th, 1790.

MOSES SEIXAS.

---

1. From *Blind Children* (London: Heinemann).

BRITISH CITIZENSHIP

B RITISH patriotism is not the mediaeval demand that the citizens of any one country all think alike, that they be of the same blood, or that they even speak the same language. Britain's mild sovereignty respects the personality of the ethnic groups found within the borders of its world-wide dominion; nay, it fosters the linguistic heritage, the national individuality even, of Irishman and Welshman, of French Canadian and Afrikander Boer, and encourages them all to develop along their own lines. Any one, therefore, who deems that patriotism exacts from him the purposeless sacrifice of his religious tradition and historic memory—that man is an alien in spirit to the Anglo-Saxon genius, and is unworthy of his British citizenship.

J. H. HERTZ, 1915.

THE RUSSIAN JEW

1

SCIENTISTS tell us that coal is nothing but concentrated sunlight. Primeval forests that for years out of number had been drinking in the rays of the sun, having been buried beneath the ground and excluded from the reviving touch of light and air, were gradually turned into coal —black, rugged, shapeless, yet retaining all its pristine energy, which, when released, provides us with light and heat. The story of the Russian Jew is the story of the coal. Under a surface marred by oppression and persecution he has accumulated immense stores of energy, in which we may find an unlimited supply of light and heat for our minds and our hearts. All we need is to discover the process, long known in the case of coal, of transforming latent strength into living power.

I. FRIEDLANDER, 1915.

1. From *History of the Jews in Poland and Russia* (London: G. P. Putnam's Sons).

YIDDISH

1

I HAVE never been able to understand how it is that a language spoken by perhaps more than half of the Jewish race should be regarded with such horror, as though it were a crime. Six million speakers are sufficient to give historic dignity to any language! One great writer alone is enough to make it holy and immortal. Take Norwegian. It is the language of only two million people. But it has become immortal through the great literary achievements of Ibsen. And even though Yiddish cannot boast of so great a writer as Ibsen, it has reason to be proud of numerous smaller men—poets, romancers, satirists, dramatists.

The main point is that Yiddish incorporates the essence of a life which is distinctive and unlike any other. There is nothing of holiness in any of the outer expressions of life. The one and only thing holy is the *human soul*, which is the source and fount of all human effort.

ISRAEL ZANGWILL, 1906.

THERE is probably no other language in existence on which so much opprobrium has been heaped as on Yiddish. Such a bias can be explained only as a manifestation of a general prejudice against everything Jewish.

126

LEO WIENER, 1899.

1. From *The Jewish World*, London.

RUSSO-JEWISH
EDUCATION

A MONG the Jews of Poland and Russia there was no learned estate, not because there were no scholars, but because the people itself was a nation of students. The ideal type for the Russian Jew was the *Lamdan*, the scholar. The highest ambition of the Russian Jew was that his sons, and if he had only daughters, that his sons-in-law should be *Lomdim*; and the greatest achievement of a man's life was his ability to provide sufficiently for them, so that, relieved from economic cares, they might devote themselves unrestrictedly to Jewish learning. To be sure, this learning was one-sided. Yet it was both wide and deep, for it embraced the almost boundless domain of religious Hebrew literature, and involved the knowledge of one of the most complicated systems of law. The knowledge of the Hebrew prayers and the Five Books of Moses would not have been sufficient to save the Russian Jew from the most terrible opprobrium—that of being an *Am-Haaretz*, an ignoramus. The ability to understand a Talmudic text, which demands years of preparation, was the minimum requirement for one who wanted to be of any consequence in the community.

I. FRIEDLANDER, 1913.

PASSOVER IN OLD RUSSIA

1

THE Passover season, when we celebrated our deliverance from
the land of Egypt, and felt so glad and thankful as if it had only just
happened, was the time our Gentile neighbours chose to remind us that
Russia was another Egypt. It was not so bad within the Pale; but in
Russian cities, and even more in the country districts, where Jewish
families lived scattered by special permission of the police, who were
always changing their minds about letting them stay, the Gentiles made
the Passover a time of horror for the Jews. Somebody would start up
that lie about murdering Christian children, and the stupid peasants
would get mad about it, and fill themselves with vodka, and set out to
kill the Jews. They attacked them with knives and clubs, and scythes
and axes, killed them or tortured them, and burned their houses. This
was called a 'pogrom'. Jews who escaped the pogroms came with
wounds on them, and horrible, horrible stories of little babies torn limb
from limb before their mother's eyes. Only to hear these things made
one sob and sob and choke with pain. People who saw such things
never smiled any more, no matter how long they lived; and sometimes
their hair turned white in a day, and some people became insane on
the spot.
MARY ANTIN, 1911.

129

1. From *The Promised Land* (London: Heinemann).

THE POGROM OCTOBER, 1905

I T had already lasted two days. But as nobody dined, nobody exchanged greetings, and nobody thought of winding up the clock for the night (for people slept dressed, anywhere, on lofts, in sheds, or in empty railway carriages), all notion of time had disappeared. People only heard the incessant jingling of broken glass-panes. At this terrible sound, the arms stiffened and the eyes became distended with fright.

Some distant houses were burning. Along the red-tinted street with the red pavement, there ran by a red man, whilst another red man stretched his arm, and from the tips of his fingers there broke forth quickly a sharp, snapping, cracking sound—and the running man dropped down.

A strange, sharp cry, 'They are shoo-ooting!' passed along the street.

Invisible and inexorable demons made their appearance. Houses and nurseries were broken in. Old men had their arms fractured; women's white bosoms were trampled upon by heavy, dirty heels. Many were perishing by torture; others were burnt alive.

Two persons were hiding in a dark cellar; an old man with his son, a schoolboy. The old man went up and opened the outer door again, to make the place look deserted by the owners. A merchant had run in. He wept, not from fear but from feeling himself in security.

'I have a son like you', he said, tearfully.

He then breathed heavily and nervously, and added reflectively, 'Like you, my boy, yes!'

The master of the house caught the merchant by his elbow, pulled him close to himself, and whispered into his ear:

'Hush! They might hear us!'

There they stood, expectant. Now and then, a rustling; an even, sleepless breathing could be heard. The brain cannot familiarize itself with these sounds in the darkness and silence. Perhaps they were asleep, none could tell.

At night—it must have been late at night—another two stole in quietly.

'Is it you?' asked one of them, without seeing anybody, and the sudden sound of his voice seemed to light up the darkness for a moment.

'Yes', answered the schoolboy. 'It's all right!'

'Hush! They might hear you', said the owner of the cellar, catching each of them by the arm and pulling them down.

The new-comers placed themselves by the wall, while one of them was rubbing his forehead with his hand.

'What is the matter?' asked the schoolboy in a whisper.

'It is blood.'

Then they grew silent. The injured man applied a handkerchief to his wound, and became quiet. There followed again a thick silence, untroubled by time. Again a sleepless breathing!

On the top, underneath the ceiling, a very faint whiteness appeared. The schoolboy was asleep, but the other four raised their heads and looked up. They looked long, for about half an hour, so that their muscles were aching through the protracted craning of their necks. At last it became clear that it was a tiny little window through which dawn peeped in.

Then hasty, frightened steps were heard, and there appeared a tall, coatless man, followed by a woman with a baby in her arms. The dawn was advancing, and one could read the expression of wild fear that stamped itself upon their faces.

'This way! This way!' whispered the man.

'They are running after us, they are looking out for us', said the woman. Her shoes were put on her bare feet, and her young body displayed strange, white, malignant spots, reminding one of a corpse.

'They won't find us; but, for God's sake, be quiet!'

'They are close by in the courtyard. Oh! be quiet, be quiet....'

The wounded man got hold of the merchant and the owner by the hand, while the merchant seized the man who had no coat. There they stood, forming a live chain, looking on at the mother with her baby.

All of a sudden there broke out a strange though familiar sound, so close and doomful. What doom it foreboded they felt at once, but their brains were loath to believe it.

The sound was repeated. It was the cry of the infant. The merchant made a kindly face and said: 'Baby is crying....'

'Lull him, my dear', said he, rushing to the mother. 'You will cause the death of us all.'

Everybody's chest and throat gasped with faintness. The mother marched up and down the cellar lulling and coaxing.

'You must not cry; sleep, my golden one ... It is I, your mother ... my heart....'

But the child cried on obstinately, wildly. There must have been something in the mother's face that was not calculated to produce a tranquilizing effect.

And now, in this warm and strange underground atmosphere, the woman's brain wrenched out a wild, mad, idea. It seemed to her that she had read it in the eyes, in the suffering silence of these unknown people. And these unhappy, frightened men understood that she was thinking of them. They understood it by the unutterably mournful tenderness with which she chanted, while drinking in the infant's eyes with her own.

'He will soon fall asleep. I know. It is always like that; he cries for a moment, then he falls asleep at once. He is a very quiet boy.' She addressed the tall man with a painful, insinuating smile. From outside there broke in a distant noise. Then came a thud, and a crack, shaking the air.

'They are searching', whispered the schoolboy.

But the infant went on crying hopelessly.

'He will undo us all', blurted out the tall man.

'I shall not give him away ... no, never!' ejaculated the distracted mother.

'O God', whispered the merchant, and covered his face with his hands. His hair was unkempt after a sleepless night. The tall man stared at the infant with fixed, protruding eyes....

'I don't know you', the woman uttered, low and crossly, on catching that fixed look. 'Who are you? What do you want of me?'

She rushed to the other men, but everybody drew back from her with fear. The infant was crying on, piercing the brain with its shouting.

'Give it to me', said the merchant, his right eyebrow trembling. 'Children like me.'

All of a sudden it grew dark in the cellar; somebody had approached the little window and was listening. At this shadow, breaking in so suddenly, they all grew quiet. They felt that it was coming, it was near, and that not another second must be lost.

The mother turned round. She stood up on her toes, and with high, uplifted arms she handed over her child to the merchant. It seemed to her that by this gesture she was committing a terrible crime ... that hissing voices were cursing her, rejecting her from heaven for ever and ever....

Strange to say, finding itself in the thick, clumsy, but loving hands of the merchant, the child grew silent.

But the mother interpreted this silence differently. In sight of everybody the woman grew grey in a single moment, as if they had poured some acid over her hair. And as soon as the child's cry died away, there resounded another cry, more awful, more shattering and heart-rending.

The mother rose up on her toes; and grey, terrible, like the goddess of justice herself, she howled in a desperate, inhuman voice that brought destruction with it.... Nobody had expected that sudden madness. The schoolboy fell in a swoon.

Afterwards, the newspapers reported details of the killing of six men and an infant by the mob; for none had dared to touch the mad old woman of twenty-six.

OSSIP DYMOV, 1906.

UNDER THE ROMANOFFS

THE plaything of a heartless bureaucracy, the natural prey of all the savage elements of society, loaded with fetters in one place, and in another driven out like some wild beast, the Russian Jew finds that for him, at least, life is composed of little else than bitterness, suffering, and degradation.

For magnitude and gloom the tragical situation has no parallel in history. Some six millions of human beings are unceasingly subjected to a State-directed torture which is both destructive and demoralizing, and constitutes at once a crime against humanity and an international perplexity.

LUCIEN WOLF, 1912.

EACH crime that wakes in man the beast,
 Is visited upon his kind.
 The lust of mobs, the greed of priest,
 The tyranny of kings, combined
 To root his seed from earth again,
 His record is one cry of pain.

Coward? Not he, who faces death,

Who singly against worlds has fought,
For what? A name he may not breathe,
For liberty of prayer and thought.
EMMA LAZARUS, 1882.

'SOLDIERS OF NICHOLAS'

1

THERE was one thing the Gentiles might do to me worse than burning or rending. It was what was done to unprotected Jewish children who fell into the hands of priests or nuns. They might baptize me. That would be worse than death by torture. Every Jewish child had that feeling. There were stories by the dozen of Jewish boys who were kidnapped by the Czar's agents and brought up in Gentile families till they were old enough to enter the army, where they served until forty years of age; and all those years the priests tried, by bribes and daily tortures, to force them to accept baptism, but in vain. This was the time of Nicholas I.

Some of these 'soldiers of Nicholas', as they were called, were taken as little boys of seven or eight—snatched from their mothers' laps. They were carried to distant villages, where their friends could never trace them, and turned over to some dirty, brutal peasant, who used them like slaves, and kept them with the pigs. No two were ever left together; and they were given false names, so that they were entirely cut off from their own world. And then the lonely child was turned over to the priests, and he was flogged and starved and terrified—a little helpless boy who cried for his mother; but still he refused to be baptized. The priests promised him good things to eat, fine clothes, and freedom from labour; but the boy turned away, and said his prayers secretly—the Hebrew prayers.

As he grew older, severer tortures were invented for him; still he refused baptism. By this time he had forgotten his mother's face, and of his prayers perhaps only the 'Shema' remained in his memory; but he was a Jew, and nothing would make him change. After he entered the army, he was bribed with promises of promotions and honours. He remained a private, and endured the cruellest discipline. When he was discharged, at the age of forty, he was a broken man, without a home, without a clue to his origin, and he spent the rest of his life wandering among Jewish settlements, searching for his family, hiding the scars of torture under his rags, begging his way from door to door.

There were men in our town whose faces made you old in a minute. They had served Nicholas I, and come back, unbaptized.

MARY ANTIN, 1911.

---

1. From *The Promised Land* (London: Heinemann).

BONTZYE SHWEIG
(BONTZYE THE SILENT)

1

DOWN here, in this world, Silent Bontzye's death made no impression at all. Ask any one you like who Bontzye was, how he lived, and what he died of; whether of heart failure, or whether his strength gave out, or whether his back broke under a heavy load, and they won't know. Perhaps, after all, he died of hunger.

Bontzye lived quietly and died quietly. He passed through our world like a shadow. He lived like a little dun-coloured grain of sand on the sea-shore, among millions of his kind; and when the wind lifted him and blew him over to the other side of the sea, nobody noticed it. When he was alive, the mud in the street preserved no impression of his feet; after his death the wind overturned the little board on his grave. The grave-digger's wife found it a long way off from the spot, and boiled a potful of potatoes over it. Three days after that, the grave-digger had forgotten where he had laid him.

A shadow! His likeness remained photographed in nobody's brain, in nobody's heart; not a trace of him remained.

'No kith, no kin!' He lived and died alone.

Had the world been less busy, some one might have remarked that Bontzye (also a human being) went about with two extinguished eyes and fearfully hollow cheeks; that even when he had no load on his shoulders his head drooped earthward as though, while yet alive, he were looking for his grave. When they carried Bontzye into the hospital, his corner in the underground lodging was soon filled—there were ten of his like waiting for it, and they put it up for auction among themselves. When they carried him from the hospital bed to the dead-house, there were twenty poor sick persons waiting for the bed. When he had been taken out of the dead-house, they brought in twenty bodies from under a building that had fallen in. Who knows how long he will rest in his grave? Who knows how many are waiting for the little plot of ground?

A quiet birth, a quiet life, a quiet death, and a quieter burial.

But it was not so in the Other World. There Bontzye's death made a great impression.

The blast of the great Messianic Shofar sounded through all the seven heavens; Bontzye Shweig has left the earth! The largest angels with the broadest wings flew about and told one another; Bontzye Shweig is to take his seat in the Heavenly Academy! In Paradise there was a noise and a joyful tumult: Bontzye Shweig! Just fancy! Bontzye Shweig!

Little child-angels with sparkling eyes, gold thread-work wings, and silver slippers, ran delightedly to meet him. The rustle of the wings, the clatter of the little slippers, and the merry laughter of the fresh, rosy mouths, filled all the heavens and reached to the Throne of Glory. Abraham our father stood in the gate, his right hand stretched out with a hearty greeting, and a sweet smile lit up his old face.

What are they wheeling through heaven? Two angels are pushing a golden arm-chair into Paradise for Bontzye Shweig.

What flashed so brightly? They were carrying past a gold crown set with precious stones all for Bontzye Shweig.

'Before the decision of the Heavenly Court has been given?' ask the saints, not quite without jealousy. 'Oh', reply the angels, 'that will be a mere formality. Even the prosecutor won't say a word against Bontzye Shweig. The case will not last five minutes.' Just consider! Bontzye Shweig!

All this time, Bontzye, just as in the other world, was too frightened to speak. He is sure it is all a dream, or else simply a mistake. He dared not raise his eyes, lest the dream should vanish, lest he should wake up in some cave full of snakes and lizards. He was afraid to speak, afraid to move, lest he should be recognized and flung into the pit. He trembles and does not hear the angels' compliments, does not see how they dance round him, makes no answer to the greeting of Abraham our father, and when he is led into the presence of the Heavenly Court he does not even wish it 'Good morning!' He is beside himself with terror. 'Who knows what rich man, what rabbi, what saint, they take me for? He will come—and that will be the end of me!' His terror is such, he never even hears the president call out: 'The case of Bontzye Shweig!' adding, as he hands the deeds to the advocate, 'Read, but make haste!'

The whole hall goes round and round in Bontzye's eyes; there is a rushing in his ears. And through the rushing he hears more and more clearly the voice of the advocate, speaking sweetly as a violin.

'His name', he hears, 'fitted him like the dress made for a slender figure by the hand of an artist-tailor.'

'What is he talking about?' wondered Bontzye, and he heard an impatient voice break in with: 'No similes, please!'

'He never', continued the advocate, 'was heard to complain of either God or man; there was never a flash of hatred in his eye; he never lifted it with a claim on heaven.'

Still Bontzye does not understand, and once again the hard voice interrupts: 'No rhetoric, please!'

'Job gave way—this one was more unfortunate.'

'Facts, dry facts.'

'He kept silent', the advocate went on, 'even when his mother died and he was given a stepmother at thirteen years old—a serpent, a vixen.'

'Can they mean me after all?' thought Bontzye.

'No insinuations against a third party', said the president, angrily.

'She grudged him every mouthful—stale, mouldy bread, tendons instead of meat—and she drank coffee with cream.'

'Keep to the subject', ordered the president.

'She grudged him everything but her finger-nails, and his black and blue body showed through the holes in his torn and fusty clothes. Winter time, in the hardest frost, he had to chop wood for her, barefoot in the yard; and his hands were too young and too weak, the logs too thick, the hatchet too blunt. But he kept silent, even to his father.'

'To that drunkard?' laughs the accuser, and Bontzye feels cold in every limb.

'And always alone', he continued; 'no playmates, no school, nor teaching of any kind—never a whole garment—never a free moment.'

'Facts, please!' reminded the president.

'He kept silent even later, when his father seized him by the hair in a fit of drunkenness and flung him out into the street on a snowy winter's night. He quietly picked himself up out of the snow and ran whither his feet carried him. He kept silent all the way to the great town—however hungry he might be, he only begged with his eyes. Bathed in a cold sweat, crushed under heavy loads, his empty stomach convulsed with hunger—he kept silent. Bespattered with mud, spat at, driven with his load off the pavement and into the road among the cabs, carts, and tramways, looking death in the eyes every moment. He never calculated the difference between other people's lot and his own—he kept silent. And he never insisted loudly on his pay; he stood in the doorway like a beggar, with a dog-like pleading in his eyes—'Come again later!' and he went like a shadow to come again later, and beg for his wage more humbly than before. He kept silent even when they cheated him of part, or threw in a false coin.

'He took everything in silence.'

'They mean me after all', thought Bontzye.

'Once', continued the advocate, after a sip of water, 'a change came into his life: there came flying along a carriage on rubber tires, drawn by two runaway horses. The driver already lay some distance off on the pavement with a cracked skull, the terrified horses foamed at the mouth, sparks shot from their hoofs, their eyes shone like fiery lamps on a winter's night—and in the carriage, more dead than alive, sat a man.

'And Bontzye stopped the horses. And the man he had saved was a charitable Jew who was not ungrateful. He put the dead man's whip into Bontzye's hands, and Bontzye became a coachman. More than that, he was provided with a wife. And Bontzye kept silent!'

'Me, they mean me!' Bontzye assured himself again, and yet had not the courage to give a glance at the Heavenly Court.

He listens to the advocate further:

'He kept silent also when his protector became bankrupt and did not pay him his wages. He kept silent when his wife ran away from him.'

'Me, they mean me!' Now he is sure of it.

'He kept silent even', began the angelic advocate once more in a still softer and sadder voice, 'when the same philanthropist paid all his creditors their due but him—and even when (riding once again in a carriage with rubber tires and fiery horses) he knocked Bontzye down and drove over him. He kept silent even in the hospital, where one may cry out. He kept silent when the doctor would not come to his bedside without being paid fifteen kopeks, and when the attendant demanded another five—for changing his linen.

'He kept silent in the death struggle—silent in death.

'Not a word against God; not a word against men!

'Dixi!'

Once more Bontzye trembled all over. He knew that after the advocate comes the prosecutor. Who knows what he will say? Bontzye himself remembered nothing of his life. Even in the other world he forgot every moment what had happened in the one before. The advocate had recalled everything to his mind. Who knows what the prosecutor will not remind him of?

'Gentlemen', begins the prosecutor, in a voice biting and acid as vinegar—but he breaks off.

'Gentlemen', he begins again, but his voice is milder, and a second time he breaks off.

Then from out the same throat comes in a voice that is almost gentle: 'Gentlemen! He was silent! I will be silent too!'

There is a hush—and there sounds in front a new, soft, trembling voice: 'Bontzye, my child!' It speaks like a harp. 'My dear child, Bontzye!'

And Bontzye's heart melts within him. Now he would lift up his eyes, but they are blinded with tears; he never felt such sweet emotion before. 'My child! Bontzye!'—no one, since his mother died, had spoken to him with such words in such a voice.

'My child', continues the presiding judge, 'you have suffered and kept silent; there is no whole limb, no whole bone in your body without a scar, without a wound, not a fibre of your soul that has not bled—and you kept silent. There they did not understand. Perhaps you yourself did not know that you might have cried out, and that at your

143

cry the walls of Jericho would have shaken and fallen. You yourself knew nothing of your hidden power.

'In the other world your silence was not understood, but that is the World of Delusion; in the World of Truth you will receive your reward. The Heavenly Court will not judge you; the Heavenly Court will not pass sentence on you; they will not apportion you a reward. Take what you will! Everything is yours.'

Bontzye looks up for the first time. He is dazzled; everything shines and flashes and streams with light.

'*Taki*—really?' he asks, shyly.

'Yes, really!' answers the presiding judge, with decision; 'really, I tell you, everything is yours; everything in heaven belongs to you. Because all that shines and sparkles is only the reflection of your hidden goodness, a reflection of your soul. You only take of what is yours.'

'*Taki?*' asks Bontzye again, this time in a firmer voice.

'*Taki!* taki! taki!' they answer from all sides.

'Well, if it is so', Bontzye smiles, 'I would like to have every day, for breakfast, a hot roll with fresh butter.'

The Court and the angels looked down, a little ashamed; the prosecutor laughed.

J. L. PERETZ, 1894. (*Trans. Helena Frank.*)

---

1. From *Stories and Pictures* (Jewish Publication Society, Philadelphia).

THE WATCH ON
THE JORDAN
(ZIONIST HYMN)

1

LIKE the crash of the thunder
Which splitteth asunder
The flame of the cloud,
On our ears ever falling
A voice is heard calling
From Zion aloud.
'Let your spirits' desires
For the land of your sires
Eternally burn;
From the foe to deliver
Our own holy river,
To Jordan return.'
Where the soft-flowing stream
Murmurs low as in dream
There set we our watch!
Our watchword, 'The sword
Of our land and our Lord';
By Jordan then set we our watch.
Rest in peace, lovéd land,
For we rest not, but stand,
Off-shaken our sloth.

When the bolts of war rattle,
To shirk not the battle
We make thee our oath.
As we hope for a heaven,
Thy chains shall be riven,
Thine ensign unfurled.
And in pride of our race
We will fearlessly face
The might of the world.
When our trumpet is blown,
And our standard is flown,
Then set we our watch!
Our watchword, 'The sword
Of our land and our Lord';
By Jordan then set we our watch.
Yea, as long as there be
Birds in air, fish in sea,
And blood in our veins;
And the lions in might,
Leaping down from the height,
Shaking, roaring, their manes;
And the dew nightly laves,
The forgotten old graves
Where Judah's sires sleep;
We swear, who are living,
To rest not in striving,
To pause not to weep.
Let the trumpet be blown,
Let the standard be flown,
Now set we our watch;
Our watchword, 'The sword
Of our land and our Lord';
In Jordan now set we our watch.
N. H. IMBER. (*Trans. I. Zangwill.*)

---

1. From *Children of the Ghetto* (London: Heinemann).

THE TRAGEDY OF
ASSIMILATION

W HAT I understand by assimilation is loss of identity. It is this
kind of assimilation, with the terrible consequences indicated,
that I dread most—even more than pogroms.

It *is* a tragedy to see a great, ancient people, distinguished for its
loyalty to its religion, and its devotion to its sacred Law, losing thousands every day by the mere process of attrition. It *is* a tragedy to see a
language held sacred by all the world, in which Holy Writ was composed, which served as the depository of Israel's greatest and best
thoughts, doomed to oblivion. It *is* a tragedy to see the descendants of
those who revealed religion to the world, and who developed the greatest religious literature in existence, so little familiar with real Jewish
thought that they have no other interpretation to offer of Israel's Scriptures, Israel's religion, and Israel's ideals and aspirations and hopes,
than those suggested by their natural opponents, slavishly following
their opinions, copying their phrases, and repeating their catchwords.
I am not accusing anybody. I am only stating facts. We are helpless
spectators of the Jewish soul wasting away before our very eyes.

Now, the rebirth of Israel's national consciousness and the revival
of Judaism are inseparable. When Israel found itself, it found its God.
When Israel lost itself, or began to work at its self-effacement, it was
sure to deny its God. The selection of Israel, the indestructibility of
God's covenant with Israel, the immortality of Israel as a nation, and

the final restoration of Israel to Palestine, where the nation will live a holy life, on holy ground, with all the wide-reaching consequences of the conversion of humanity, and the establishment of the Kingdom of God on earth—all these are the common ideals and the common ideas that permeate the whole of Jewish literature extending over nearly four thousand years.

S. SCHECHTER, 1906.

THERE has been one short period in modern Jewish history when Israel grew utterly weary of toil and trouble, and began to take pleasure in the fleeting hour, as other nations do. But this was a mere passing phase, a temporary loss of consciousness. The prophetic spirit cannot be crushed, except for a time. It comes to life again, and masters the Prophet in his own despite. So, too, the prophetic People regained consciousness in its own despite. The Spirit that called Moses thousands of years ago and sent him on his mission, against his own will, now calls again the generation of to-day, saying, '*And that which cometh into your mind shall not be at all; in that ye say, We will be as the nations ... As I live, saith the Lord God, surely with a mighty hand ... will I be king over you.*'

ACHAD HA'AM, 1904. (*Trans. Leon Simon.*)

THE VALLEY OF
DRY BONES

T HE hand of the Lord was upon me, and the Lord carried me out in a spirit, and set me down in the midst of the valley, and it was full of bones; and He caused me to pass by them round about, and, behold, there were very many in the open valley; and, lo, they were very dry. And He said unto me: 'Son of man, can these bones live?' And I answered: 'O Lord God, Thou knowest'. Then he said unto me: 'Prophesy over these bones, and say unto them: O ye dry bones, hear the word of the Lord: Thus saith the Lord God unto these bones: Behold, I will cause breath to enter into you, and ye shall live. And I will lay sinews upon you, and will bring up flesh upon you, and cover you with skin, and put breath in you, and ye shall live; and ye shall know that I am the Lord.' So I prophesied as I was commanded; and as I prophesied, there was a noise, and behold a commotion, and the bones came together, bone to its bone. And I beheld, and, lo, there were sinews upon them, and flesh came up, and skin covered them above; but there was no breath in them. Then said He unto me: 'Prophesy unto the breath, prophesy, son of man, and say to the breath: Thus saith the Lord God: Come from the four winds, O breath, and breathe upon these slain, that they may live.' So I prophesied as He commanded me, and the breath came into them, and they lived, and stood up upon their feet, an exceeding great host. Then He said unto me: 'Son of man, these bones are the whole house of Israel; behold, they say: Our bones are dried up, and our hope is lost: we are clean cut off. Therefore prophesy, and say unto them: Thus saith the Lord God: Behold, I will open your graves, and cause you to come up out of your graves, O My people; and I will bring you into the Land of Israel. And ye shall know that I am the Lord, when I have opened your graves, and caused you to come up out of your graves, O My people. And I will put My spirit in you, and ye shall live, and I will place you in your own land; and ye shall know that I the Lord have spoken, and performed it, saith the Lord.'

EZEKIEL 37. 1–14.

PALESTINE

THE very name Palestine stirs within us the most elevated sentiments. There is no country, no matter how important in itself, to which such sublime memories attach themselves. From our earliest youth, our imagination, nourished on the sacred traditions of the Hebrew Scriptures, loves to transport itself to those heights where of old pious souls heard in each echo the voice of God, where each stone is a symbol of divine revelation, each ruin a monument of divine anger. The followers of three religions turn with veneration towards these ruins of 2,000 years. All find consolation in that land, some by its memories, others by its hopes. Even sceptics are ready to render historic justice to the great events of which it was the theatre: thus the description of this land and its story have a palpitating interest for all.

S. MUNK, 1863.

THE LAST CORPSES IN THE DESERT

U P, wanderers in the wild, and come away!
      Long is the journey yet and long the fray.
Enough of roving now in desert places—
There lies a great, wide road before your faces.
But forty years of wandering have sped,
And yet we leave six hundred thousand dead.
Dishonoured let them lie, across the pack
They bore from out of Egypt on their back.
Sweet be their dreams of garlic and of leek,
Of flesh-pots wide, of fatty steam and reek.
Around the last dead slave, maybe to-night,
The desert wind with desert beast shall fight,
And joyously to-morrow's dawning shine
Upon the firstlings of a mighty line,
And lest the sands with all their sleepers start,
Let each man's footfall sound but in his heart.
Let each man in his heart hear God's voice say:
'A new land's border shalt thou cross to-day!
'No more the quails from heav'n, no more light bread—
The bread of toil, fruit of the hands, instead.
'No more wild tents pitched under heaven's dome—
Another kind shall ye set up for home.

'Beneath His sky, the wilderness outside,
God has another world that reaches wide,
'Beyond the howling desert with its sand,
There waits beneath His stars the Promised Land.'
CH. N. BYALIK, 1896. (*Trans. Helena Frank.*)

ZIONISM

O NE thing is to me certain, high above any doubt: the movement will continue. I know not when I shall die, but Zionism will never die.

THEODOR HERZL, 1898.

ZIONISM is the lineal heir of the attachment to Zion which led the Babylonian exiles under Zerubbabel to rebuild the Temple, and which flamed up in the heroic struggle of the Maccabees against Antiochus Epiphanes. The idea that it is a set-back of Jewish history is a controversial fiction. The great bulk of the Jewish people have throughout their history remained faithful to the dream of a restoration of their national life in Judea. The Zionist movement is to-day the greatest popular movement that Jewish history has ever known.

LUCIEN WOLF, 1910, *in Encyclopaedia Britannica.*

ALL over the world Jews are resolved that our common Judaism shall not be crushed out by short-sighted fanatics for local patriotism; and, in so far as Zionism strengthens this sense of the solidarity of our common Judaism, we are all Zionists.

I. ABRAHAMS, 1905.

THE BRITISH DECLARATION
ON PALESTINE

NOVEMBER 2, 1917—APRIL 24, 1920

ENGLAND, great England, whose gaze sweeps over all the seas—free England—will understand and sympathize with the aims and aspirations of Zionism.

THEODOR HERZL, 1900.

FOR the first time since the days of Cyrus, a great Government has hailed the Jews as one among the family of nations. This is much more than a Jewish triumph. It is a triumph for civilization and for humanity. It will mean releasing for mankind, as a great spiritual force, the soul of our people.

JEWISH CHRONICLE, NOVEMBER 9, 1917.

A LAND focuses a people, and calls forth, as nothing else can, its spiritual potentialities. The resurrection of the Jewish nation on its own soil will reopen its sacred fountains of creative energy. Remember the days of old. After the proclamation issued by Cyrus, the mass of the Jewish people still remained in Babylon. All told only 42,000 men, women, and children took advantage of the king's proclamation and followed Ezra back to Zion, the land of their fathers. But compare the contribution to civilization made by these men with that of their brethren who remained in the Dispersion. The handful of 'Zionists' and their descendants, because living on their own soil, changed the entire future of mankind. They edited and collected the Prophets, wrote some of the fairest portions of the Scriptures, formed the canon of the Bible, and gave the world its monotheistic religions. As in the days of Cyrus, the overwhelming majority of Jews of to-day will continue to live where they now are, praying and working in absolute loyalty for the land of their birth or adoption, and ever beholding their peace in its welfare. Only a remnant shall return. But it is the national rejuvenation of that remnant that will open a new chapter in the annals of the human spirit.

J. H. HERTZ, 1917.

FOR millions of poor and hundreds of thousands of prosperous Jews Mr. Balfour's announcement had the serene sound of a long-expected Messianic message. The day that witnessed Great Britain's decision to stake the whole of the Empire's power in the Jewish cause is one which can never be blotted out from the world's history.

MAXIMILIAN HARDEN, 1917.

JUDAISM AND THE
NEW JUDEA

I

THE return to Zion must be preceded by our return to Judaism.
THEODOR HERZL, 1897.

ISRAEL is a nation by reason only of his religion, by his possession of the Torah.
SAADYAH GAON, 933.

ISRAEL, to the Rabbis at least, is not a nation by virtue of race or of certain peculiar political combinations. The brutal Torah-less nationalism promulgated in certain quarters would have been to them just as hateful as the suicidal Torah-less universalism preached in other quarters. And if we could imagine for a moment Israel giving up its allegiance to God, its Torah, and its divine institution, the Rabbis would be the first to sign its death warrant as a nation.
S. SCHECHTER, 1909.

WE will return to Zion as we went forth, bringing back the faith we carried away with us.

MORDECAI M. NOAH, 1824.

II

ISRAEL'S contribution to the common treasure of humanity will ever be primarily religious. Wide sympathy, ready help, and absolute self-determination must therefore be accorded in the New Judea to Jewish religious learning, Jewish religious institutions, and Jewish religious life. They alone contain the secret of Israel's immortality. The story of Israel's ancient kinsmen—Moab, Ammon, Edom—though these remained on their own soil, loses itself in the sands of the desert, while the story of Israel issues in eternity. Why? Israel alone had the Torah, and it is that which endowed him with deathlessness. And Israel will remain deathless—as long as Israel continues to cling to the Torah. Without the Torah, Israel's story will also lose itself in the sands of the desert, *even on its own soil.*

The New Judea must be the spiritual descendant of old Judea, and the mission of Judea, new or old, is first of all to be Judea.

J. H. HERTZ, 1918.

I LIKE to think of Jewish History as standing ever at the centre point of its path—having as much to look forward to as to look back upon; and the events of to-day, with their special message to Israel, must surely fortify us in this view, and speed us to make good our efforts for our people and for the nations.

A. EICHHOLZ, 1917.

THE TESTIMONY
OF THE NATIONS

ENGLAND, awake! awake! awake!
    Jerusalem thy sister calls.
    Why wilt thou sleep the sleep of death
    And close her from thy ancient walls?
    Thy hills and valleys felt her feet
    Gently upon their bosoms move;
    Thy gates beheld sweet Zion's ways:
    Then was a time of joy and love.
    WILLIAM BLAKE.

WORLD'S DEBT TO ISRAEL

W E Gentiles owe our life to Israel. It is Israel who has brought us the message that God is one, and that God is a just and righteous God, and demands righteousness of his children, and demands nothing else. It is Israel that has brought us the message that God is our Father. It is Israel who, in bringing us the divine law, has laid the foundation of liberty. It is Israel who had the first free institutions the world ever saw. It is Israel who has brought us our Bible, our prophets, our apostles. When sometimes our own unchristian prejudices flame out against the Jewish people, let us remember that all that we have and all that we are we owe, under God, to what Judaism has given us.

LYMAN ABBOTT.

AT a time when the deepest night of inhumanity covered the rest of mankind, the religion of Israel breathed forth a spirit of love and brotherhood which must fill even the stranger, if he be only willing to see, with reverence and admiration. Israel has given the world true humanitarianism, just as it has given the world the true God.

C. H. CORNILL, 1895.

ISRAEL AND HIS
REVELATION

THE religion of the Bible is well said to be *revealed*, because the great natural truth, that 'righteousness tendeth to life', is seized and exhibited there with such incomparable force and efficacy. All, or very nearly all, the nations of mankind have recognized the importance of conduct, and have attributed to it a natural obligation. They, however, looked at conduct, not as something full of happiness and joy, but as something one could not manage to do without. But 'Zion heard of it and rejoiced, and the daughters of Judah were *glad*, because of thy judgements, O Eternal!' Happiness is our being's end and aim, and no one has ever come near Israel in feeling, and in making others feel, that to righteousness belongs happiness! As long as the world lasts, all who want to make progress in righteousness will come to Israel for inspiration, as to the people who have had the sense for righteousness most glowing and strongest.

This does truly constitute for Israel a most extra-ordinary distinction. 'God hath given commandment to bless, and He hath blessed, and we cannot reverse it; He hath not seen iniquity in Jacob, and He hath not seen perverseness in Israel; the Eternal, his God, is with him.'
MATTHEW ARNOLD, 1875.

ISRAEL, GREECE,
AND ROME

1

FOR a philosophic mind there are not more than three histories of real interest in the past of humanity: Greek history, the history of Israel, and Roman history.

Greece has an exceptional past. Our science, our arts, our literature, our philosophy, our political code, our maritime law, are of Greek origin. The framework of human culture created by Greece is susceptible of indefinite enlargement. Greece had only one thing wanting in the circle of her moral and intellectual activity, but this was an important void; she despised the humble and did not feel the need of a just God. Her philosophers, while dreaming of the immortality of the soul, were tolerant towards the iniquities of this world. Her religions were merely elegant municipal playthings.

... Israel's sages burned with anger over the abuses of the world. The prophets were fanatics in the cause of social justice, and loudly proclaimed that if the world was not just, or capable of becoming so, it had better be destroyed—a view which, if utterly wrong, led to deeds of heroism and brought about a grand awakening of the forces of humanity.

One other great humanizing force had to be created—a force powerful enough to beat down the obstacles which local patriotism offered to the idealistic propaganda of Greece and Judea. Rome fulfilled this extraordinary function. Force is not a pleasant thing to contemplate, and the recollections of Rome will never have the powerful attraction of the affairs of Greece and of Israel; but Roman history is none the less part and parcel of these histories, which are the pivot of all the rest, and which we may call providential.

ERNEST RENAN, 1887.

NONE of the resplendent names in history—Egypt, Athens, Rome—can compare in eternal grandeur with Jerusalem. For Israel has given to mankind the category of holiness. Israel alone has known the thirst for social justice, and that inner saintliness which is the source of justice.

CHARLES WAGNER, 1918.

AMONG the theocratic nations of the ancient East, the Hebrews seem to us as sober men in a world of intoxicated beings. Antiquity, however, held *them* to be the dreamers among waking folk.

H. LOTZE, 1864.

---

1. From *History of the People of Israel* (London: Chapman & Hall).

WHAT IS A JEW?

W HAT is a Jew? This question is not at all so odd as it seems. Let us see what kind of peculiar creature the Jew is, which all the rulers and all nations have together and separately abused and molested, oppressed and persecuted, trampled and butchered, burned and hanged—and in spite of all this is yet alive! What is a Jew, who has never allowed himself to be led astray by all the earthly possessions which his oppressors and persecutors constantly offered him in order that he should change his faith and forsake his own Jewish religion?

The Jew is that sacred being who has brought down from heaven the everlasting fire, and has illumined with it the entire world. He is the religious source, spring, and fountain out of which all the rest of the peoples have drawn their beliefs and their religions.

The Jew is the pioneer of liberty. Even in those olden days, when the people were divided into but two distinct classes, slaves and masters—even so long ago had the law of Moses prohibited the practice of keeping a person in bondage for more than six years.

The Jew is the pioneer of civilization. Ignorance was condemned in olden Palestine more even than it is to-day in civilized Europe. Moreover, in those wild and barbarous days, when neither life nor the death of any one counted for anything at all, Rabbi Akiba did not refrain from expressing himself openly against capital punishment, a practice which is recognized to-day as a highly civilized way of punishment.

The Jew is the emblem of civil and religious toleration. 'Love the stranger and the sojourner', Moses commands, 'because you have been strangers in the land of Egypt.' And this was said in those remote and savage times when the principal ambition of the races and nations consisted in crushing and enslaving one another. As concerns religious toleration, the Jewish faith is not only far from the missionary spirit of converting people of other denominations, but on the contrary the Talmud commands the Rabbis to inform and explain to every one who willingly comes to accept the Jewish religion, all the difficulties involved in its acceptance, and to point out to the would-be proselyte that the righteous of all nations have a share in immortality. Of such a lofty and ideal religious toleration not even the moralists of our present day can boast.

The Jew is the emblem of eternity. He whom neither slaughter nor torture of thousands of years could destroy, he whom neither fire nor sword nor inquisition was able to wipe off from the face of the earth, he who was the first to produce the oracles of God, he who has been for so long the guardian of prophecy, and who transmitted it to the rest of the world—such a nation cannot be destroyed. The Jew is everlasting as is eternity itself.

LEO TOLSTOY.

THE BOOK OF THE AGES

T HE Bible is the book of the ancient world, the book of the Middle Ages, and the book of modern times. Where does Homer stand compared with the Bible? Where the Vedas or the Koran? The Bible is inexhaustible.

A. HARNACK.

WITHIN this awful volume lies
    The mystery of mysteries:
    Happiest he of human race
    To whom God has given grace
    To read, to fear, to hope, to pray,
    To lift the latch, and learn the way;
    And better had he ne'er been born
    Who reads to doubt, or reads to scorn.
SIR WALTER SCOTT.

HOW many ages and generations have brooded and wept and agonized over this book! What untellable joys and ecstasies, what support to martyrs at the stake, from it! To what myriads has it been the shore and rock of safety—the refuge from driving tempest and wreck! Translated into all languages, how it has united this diverse world! Of its thousands there is not a verse, not a word, but is thick-studded with human emotion.

WALT WHITMAN.

THE BIBLE, THE EPIC OF
THE WORLD

1

A PART from all questions of religious and historical import, the Bible is the epic of the world. It unrolls a vast panorama in which the ages move before us in a long train of solemn imagery from the creation of the world onward. Against this gorgeous background we see mankind strutting, playing their little part on the stage of history. We see them taken from the dust and returning to the dust. We see the rise and fall of empires, we see great cities, now the hive of busy industry, now silent and desolate—a den of wild beasts. All life's fever is there, its hopes and joys, its suffering and sin and sorrow.

J. G. FRAZER, 1895.

WRITTEN in the East, these characters live for ever in the West; written in one province, they pervade the world; penned in rude times, they are prized more and more as civilization advances; product of antiquity, they come home to the business and bosoms of men, women, and children in modern days.

R. L. STEVENSON.

. . .

THE Bible thoroughly known is a literature in itself—the rarest and the richest in all departments of thought or imagination which exists.
J. A. FROUDE, 1886.

---

1. From *Passages of the Bible Chosen for their Literary Beauty* (London: A. & C. Black).

THE BIBLE IN EDUCATION

C ONSIDER the great historical fact that for three centuries this Book has been woven into the life of all that is best and noblest in English history; that it has become the national epic of Britain, and is familiar to noble and simple, from John o' Groat's to Land's End; that it is written in the noblest and purest English, and abounds in exquisite beauties of a merely literary form; and, finally, that it forbids the veriest hind who never left his village to be ignorant of the existence of other countries and other civilizations, and of a great past, stretching back to the furthest limits of the oldest nations of the world. By the study of what other book could children be so much humanized, and made to feel that each figure in that vast historical procession fills, like themselves, but a momentary space in the interval between the Eternities; and earns the blessings or the curses of all time, according to its effort to do good and hate evil?

T. H. HUXLEY, 1870.

THE greater the intellectual progress of the ages, the more fully will it be possible to employ the Bible not only as the foundation, but as the instrument, of education.

J. W. GOETHE.

THE BIBLE AND
DEMOCRACY

T HIS Bible is for the government of the people, by the people, and for the people.
  JOHN WYCLIF, *in Preface to first English Translation of the Bible*, 1384.

THROUGHOUT the history of the Western world the Scriptures have been the great instigators of revolt against the worst forms of clerical and political despotism. The Bible has been the Magna Charta of the poor and of the oppressed; down to modern times no State has had a constitution in which the interests of the people are so largely taken into account, in which the duties so much more than the privileges of rulers are insisted upon, as that drawn up for Israel in Deuteronomy and in Leviticus; nowhere is the fundamental truth that the welfare of the State, in the long run, depends on the uprightness of the citizen so strongly laid down.... The Bible is the most democratic book in the world. T. H. HUXLEY, 1892.

WHERE there is no reverence for the Bible, there can be no true refinement of manners.
  F. NIETZSCHE.

THE HEBREW LANGUAGE

A QUIVER full of steel arrows, a cable with strong coils, a trumpet of brass crashing through the air with two or three sharp notes—such is the Hebrew language. The letters of its books are not to be many, but they are to be letters of fire. A language of this sort is not destined to say much, but what it does is beaten out upon an anvil. It is to pour floods of anger and utter cries of rage against the abuses of the world, calling the four winds of heaven to the assault of the citadels of evil. Like the jubilee horn of the sanctuary it will be put to no profane use; but it will sound the notes of the holy war against injustice and the call of the great assemblies; it will have accents of rejoicing, and accents of terror; it will become the trumpet of judgement.

ERNEST RENAN, 1887.

REBECCA'S HYMN

WHEN Israel, of the Lord beloved,
    Out from the land of bondage came,
Her fathers' God before her moved,
An awful guide in smoke and flame.
By day, along the astonished lands,
The cloudy pillar glided slow;
By night, Arabia's crimsoned sands
Returned the fiery column's glow.
There rose the choral hymn of praise,
And trump and timbrel answered keen,
And Zion's daughters poured their lays,
With priest's and warrior's voice between.
No portents now our foes amaze,
Forsaken Israel wanders lone;
Our fathers would not know Thy ways,
And Thou hast left them to their own.
But present still, though now unseen!
When brightly shines the prosperous day.
Be thoughts of Thee a cloudy screen
To temper the deceitful ray.
And oh, when stoops on Judah's path
In shade and storm the frequent night,

Be Thou, long-suffering, slow to wrath,
A burning and a shining light!
Our harps we left by Babel's streams,
The tyrant's jest, the Gentile's scorn;
No censer round our altar beams,
And mute are timbrel, harp, and horn.
But Thou hast said, 'The blood of goat,
The flesh of rams, I will not prize;
A contrite heart, a humble thought,
Are Mine accepted sacrifice'.
SIR WALTER SCOTT, 1820.

MOSES

TO lead into freedom a people long crushed by tyranny; to discipline and order such a mighty host; to harden them into fighting men, before whom warlike tribes quailed and walled cities went down; to repress discontent and jealousy and mutiny; to combat reactions and reversions; to turn the quick, fierce flame of enthusiasm to the service of a steady purpose, require some towering character—a character blending in highest expression the qualities of politician, patriot, philosopher, and statesman—the union of the wisdom of the Egyptians with the unselfish devotion of the meekest of men.

The striking differences between Egyptian and Hebrew polity are not of form, but of essence. The tendency of the one is to subordination and oppression; of the other, to individual freedom. Strangest of recorded birth! From the strongest and most splendid despotism of antiquity comes the freest republic. From between the paws of the rock-hewn Sphinx rises the genius of human liberty, and the trumpets of the Exodus throb with the defiant proclamation of the rights of man.

The Hebrew commonwealth was based upon the individual—a commonwealth whose ideal it was that every man should sit under his own vine and fig-tree, with none to vex him or make him afraid; a commonwealth in which none should be condemned to ceaseless toil; in which, for even the bond slave there should be hope; in which, for even the beast of burden there should be rest. It is not the protection of property, but the protection of humanity, that is the aim of the Mosaic code. Its Sabbath day and Sabbath year secure, even to the lowliest, rest and leisure. With the blast of the jubilee trumpets the slave goes free, and a re-division of the land secures again to the poorest his fair share in the bounty of the common Creator. The reaper must leave something for the gleaner; even the ox cannot be muzzled as he treadeth out the corn. Everywhere, in everything, the dominant idea is that of our homely phrase—'Live and let live.'

That there is one day in the week that the working man may call his own, one day in the week on which the hammer is silent and the loom stands idle, is due, through Christianity, to Judaism—to the code promulgated in the Sinaitic wilderness. And who that considers the waste of productive forces can doubt that modern society would be not merely happier, but richer, had we received as well as the Sabbath day the grand idea of the Sabbath year, or, adapting its spirit to our changed conditions, secured in another way an equivalent reduction of working hours.

It is in these characteristics of the Mosaic institutions that, as in the fragments of a Colossus, we may read the greatness of the mind whose impress they bear—of a mind in advance of its surroundings, in advance of its age; of one of those star souls that dwindle not with distance, but, glowing with the radiance of essential truth, hold their light while institutions and languages and creeds change and pass.

Leader and servant of men! Law-giver and benefactor! Toiler towards the Promised Land seen only by the eye of faith! Type of the high souls who in every age have given to earth its heroes and its martyrs, whose deeds are the precious possession of the race, whose memories are its sacred heritage! With whom among the founders of Empire shall we compare him?

To dispute about the inspiration of such a man were to dispute about words. From the depths of the Unseen such characters must draw their strength; from fountains that flow only from the pure in heart must come their wisdom. Of something more real than matter; of something higher than the stars; of a light that will endure when suns are dead and dark; of a purpose of which the physical universe is but a passing phrase, such lives tell.

HENRY GEORGE, 1884.

THE BURIAL OF MOSES

B Y Nebo's lonely mountain,
    On this side Jordan's wave,
In a vale in the land of Moab,
There lies a lonely grave.
But no man built that sepulchre,
And no man saw it e'er;
For the angels of God upturned the sod
And laid the dead man there.
That was the grandest funeral
That ever passed on earth;
Yet no man heard the trampling,
Or saw the train go forth:
Noiselessly as the daylight
Comes when the night is done,
And the crimson streak on ocean's cheek
Grows into the great sun.
Perchance the bald old eagle
On grey Beth-peor's height
Out of his rocky eyrie
Looked on the wondrous sight;
Perchance the lion stalking
Still shuns that hallowed spot;

For beast and bird have seen and heard
That which man knoweth not.
This was the bravest warrior
That ever buckled sword;
This the most gifted poet
That ever breathed a word;
And never earth's philosopher
Traced with his golden pen
On the deathless page truths half so sage
As he wrote down for men.
C. F. ALEXANDER.

ISRAEL'S PSALTER

A T no period throughout the whole range of Jewish history has the poetic voice been mute. Every great fact throughout its entire course, right down to modern times, has left its impress on the Synagogue liturgy. Jewish poetry is the mirror of Jewish national life, and poetic utterance a divine instinct of the Jewish mind. For to the Hebrew, poetry was both prayer and praise, and alike in mercy and affliction the poet's words became for the Hebrew the medium of direct communion with the Divine. Adoration can rise no higher than we find it in the Psalter.

JOHN E. DOW, 1890.

THE ancient psalm still keeps its music, and this is but the outer sign of its spiritual power, which remains as near and intimate to our needs, human and divine, as in David's day. So, indeed, it seems to have remained through all the centuries—the one body of poetry which has gone on, apart from the change of races and languages, speaking with a voice of power to the hearts of men.

ERNEST RHYS, 1895.

.   .   .

THE Psalms resound, and will continue to resound, as long as there shall be men created in the image of God, in whose hearts the sacred fire of religion shines and glows; for they are religion itself put into speech.

C. H. CORNILL, 1897.

THE PSALMS IN
HUMAN LIFE

ABOVE the couch of David, according to Rabbinical tradition, there hung a harp. The midnight breeze, as it rippled over the strings, made such music that the poet king was constrained to rise from his bed, and till the dawn flushed the eastern skies he wedded words to the strains. The poetry of that tradition is condensed in the saying that the Book of Psalms contains the whole music of the heart of man, swept by the hand of his Maker. In it are gathered the lyrical burst of his tenderness, the moan of his penitence, the pathos of his sorrow, the triumph of his victory, the despair of his defeat, the firmness of his confidence, the rapture of his assured hope.

The Psalms express in exquisite words the kinship which every thoughtful human heart craves to find with a supreme, unchanging, loving God, who will be to him a protector, guardian, and friend. They translate into speech the spiritual passion of the loftiest genius; they also utter, with the beauty born of truth and simplicity, the inarticulate and humble longings of the unlettered peasant. They alone have known no limitations to a particular age, country, or form of faith. In the Psalms the vast hosts of suffering humanity have found the deepest expression of their hopes and fears.

R. E. PROTHERO, 1903.

THE SPACIOUS FIRMAMENT ON HIGH (PSALM 19)

The spacious firmament on high,
⠀⠀With all the blue ethereal sky,
And spangled heavens, a shining frame,
Their great Original proclaim.
Th' unwearied sun from day to day
Does his Creator's power display,
And publishes to every land
The work of an Almighty hand.
Soon as the evening shades prevail,
The moon takes up the wondrous tale;
And nightly to the list'ning earth,
Repeats the story of her birth:
Whilst all the stars that round her burn,
And all the planets in their turn,
Confirm the tidings as they roll,
And spread the truth from pole to pole.
What though in solemn silence all
Move round the dark terrestrial ball?
What though nor real voice nor sound
Amid their radiant orbs be found?
In reason's ear they all rejoice,

And utter forth a glorious voice;
For ever singing as they shine,
'The hand that made us is divine.'
JOSEPH ADDISON, 1719.

'O GOD, OUR HELP IN AGES PAST' (PSALM 90)

O GOD, our help in ages past,
    Our hope for years to come,
Our shelter from the stormy blast,
And our eternal home;
Beneath the shadow of Thy Throne
Thy saints have dwelt secure;
Sufficient is Thine arm alone,
And our defence is sure.
Before the hills in order stood,
Or earth received her frame,
From everlasting Thou art God,
To endless years the same.
A thousand ages in Thy sight
Are like an evening gone;
Short as the watch that ends the night
Before the rising sun.
Time, like an ever-rolling stream,
Bears all its sons away;
They fly, forgotten, as a dream
Dies at the opening day.
O God, our help in ages past,

Our hope for years to come,
Be Thou our guard while troubles last,
And our eternal home.
ISAAC WATTS, 1719.

THE LIVING POWER OF
THE JEWISH PROPHETS

T HE moral feelings of men have been deepened and strengthened, and also softened, and almost created, by the Jewish prophets. In modern times we hardly like to acknowledge the full force of their words, lest they should prove subversive to society. And so we explain them away or spiritualize them, and convert what is figurative into what is literal, and what is literal into what is figurative. And still, after all our interpretation or misinterpretation, whether due to a false theology or an imperfect knowledge of the original language, the force of the words remains, and a light of heavenly truth and love streams from them even now more than 2,500 years after they were first uttered.

BENJAMIN JOWETT.

ONE lesson, and only one, history may be said to repeat with distinctness, that the world is built somehow on moral foundations; that in the long run it is well with the good; in the long run it is ill with the wicked. But this is no science; it is no more than the old doctrine taught long ago by the Hebrew prophets.

J. A. FROUDE, 1889.

THE BOOK OF JONAH.

A N involuntary smile passes over one's features at the mention of the name of Jonah. For the popular conception sees nothing in this book but a silly tale exciting us to derision. I have read the Book of Jonah at least a hundred times, and I will publicly avow that I cannot even now take up this marvellous book, nay, nor even speak of it, without the tears rising to my eyes and my heart beating higher. This apparently trivial book is one of the deepest and grandest that was ever written, and I should like to say to every one who approaches it, 'Take off thy shoes, for the place whereon thou standest is holy ground'.

Jonah receives from God the command to go to Nineveh to proclaim the judgement, but he rose to flee from the presence of the Lord by ship unto Tarshish in the far west. From the very beginning of the narrative, the genuine and loyal devotion of the heathen seamen is placed in intentional and exceedingly powerful contrast to the behaviour of the prophet—they are the sincere believers: he is the only heathen on board. After Jonah has been saved from storm and sea by the fish, he again receives the command to go to Nineveh. He obeys; and, wonderful to relate, scarcely has the strange preacher traversed the third part of the city crying out his warning, than the whole of Nineveh proclaim a fast and put on sackcloth. The people of Nineveh believed the words of the preacher and humiliated themselves before God; therefore, the ground and motive of the Divine judgement ceased to exist: 'God repented of the evil that He thought to do them, and He did it not'. Now comes the fourth chapter, on account of which the whole book was written, and which cannot be replaced by paraphrase.

'But it' [i.e. God's determining not to destroy Nineveh because of its sincere repentance] 'displeased Jonah exceedingly, and he was angry. And he prayed unto the Lord, and said, I pray thee, O Lord, was not this my saying, when I was yet in my country? Therefore I hasted to flee unto Tarshish: for I knew that Thou art a gracious God, and full of compassion, slow to anger, and plenteous in mercy, and repentest Thee of the evil. Therefore now, O Lord, take, I beseech Thee, my life from me; for it is better for me to die than to live. And the Lord said, Doest thou well to be angry? Then Jonah went out of the city, and sat on the east side of the city, and there made him a booth, and sat under it in the shadow, till he might see what would become of the city. And the Lord God prepared a gourd and made it to come up over Jonah, that it might be a shadow over his head, to deliver him from his evil case. So Jonah was exceedingly glad because of the gourd. But God prepared a worm when the morning rose the next day, and it smote the gourd that it withered. And it came to pass, when the sun arose, that God prepared a sultry east wind; and the sun beat upon the head of Jonah, that he fainted, and requested for himself that he might die, and said, It is better for me to die than to live. And God said to Jonah, Doest thou well to be angry for the gourd? And he said, I do well to be angry even unto death. And the Lord said, Thou hast had pity on the gourd, for the which thou hast not laboured, neither madest it grow; which came up in a night and perished in a night; and should not I have pity on Nineveh, that great city; wherein are more than sixscore thousand persons that cannot discern between their right hand and their left hand; and also much cattle'?

With this question the book closes. More simply, as something quite self-evident, and therefore more sublimely and touchingly, the truth was never spoken in the Hebrew Scriptures that God, as Creator of the whole earth, must also be the God and Father of the entire world, in whose loving, kind, and fatherly heart all men are equal, before whom there is no difference of nation and creed, but only men, whom He has created in His own image.[1]

C. H. CORNILL, 1894.

I AM convinced that the Bible becomes ever more beautiful the more it is understood.

J. W. GOETHE.

---

1. The Book of Jonah, together with Isaiah 58, is the prophetical Lesson for the Day of Atonement.

JOB

I CALL the Book of Job one of the grandest things ever written with pen ... a noble book, all men's book! There is nothing, I think, in the Bible or out of it, of equal literary merit.

T. CARLYLE.

THIS extraordinary book—a book of which it is to say little to call it unequalled of its kind, and which will one day, perhaps, when it is allowed to stand on its own merits, be seen towering up alone, far away above all the poetry of the world.

J. A. FROUDE, 1885.

ECCLESIASTES

THE old cycles are for ever renewed, and it is no paradox that he who would advance can never cling too close to the past. *The thing that has been is the thing that will be again*; if we realize that, we may avoid many of the disillusions, miseries, insanities that for ever accompany the throes of new birth. Set your shoulder joyously to the world's wheel; you may spare yourself some unhappiness if, beforehand, you slip the Book of Ecclesiastes beneath your arm.

HAVELOCK ELLIS.

THE BOOK OF ESTHER

1

WITHIN it burn a lofty independence and a genuine patriotism.

The story of Esther, glorified by the genius of Handel and sanctified by the piety of Racine, not only affords material for the noblest and gentlest of meditations, but is a token that in the daily events—the unforeseen chances—of life, in little unremembered acts, God is surely present.

When Esther nerved herself to enter, at the risk of her life, the presence of Ahasuerus—'I will go in unto the king, and if I perish I perish'—when her patriotic feeling vented itself in that noble cry, 'How can I endure to see the evil that shall come unto my people? or how can I endure to see the destruction of my kindred'?—she expressed, although she never named the name of God, a religious devotion as acceptable to Him as that of Moses and David.

A. P. STANLEY, 1876.

WE search the world for truth; we cull
 The good, the pure, the beautiful
 From graven stone and written scroll,
 From all old flower-fields of the soul;
 And, weary seekers of the best,

We come back laden from our quest,
To find that all the sages said
Is in the Book our mothers read.
J. G. WHITTIER.

---

1. From *History of the Jewish Church* (London: John Murray).

THE TALMUD

T HE Talmud, which was as a second life to the men of the Ghetto, was not only a book of philosophy or devotion, it was a reservoir of national life; it was the faithful mirror of the civilization of Babylon and Judea, and, at the same time, a magical phantasmagoria of all the wild dreams, the fables, the legends, the scraps of science more or less exact, the reveries, the audacious theories discovered by the Wandering Jew in his endless travels. Every generation of Judaism had accumulated its facts and fancies there. Even the Bible itself did not come so close to the daily life of the Ghetto as the Talmud and the Mishna. The Bible was a thing eternal, apart, unchanging. The Talmud was a daily companion, living, breathing, contemporary, with a hundred remedies for a hundred needs. A nation persecuted, lives through its time of stress rather by its commentaries than by its Scriptures. In the Ghetto the Talmud was a door into the ideal always open. When the Christians burned the Jews they did no enduring harm to Judaism, for martyrdom purifies and strengthens every cause. But when they sequestrated every copy of the Talmud that fraud or force could discover, and burned the spiritual bread of a devoted people upon the public square, they committed an irreparable injury; for, by withdrawing its ideal, they debased the population of the Ghetto.

A. MARY F. ROBINSON, 1892.

THE HUMANITY OF JEWISH
WISDOM

I N my early youth I read—I have forgotten where—the words of the ancient Jewish sage—Hillel, if I remember rightly: 'If thou art not for thyself, who will be for thee? But if thou art for thyself alone, wherefore art thou'?

The inner meaning of these words impressed me with its profound wisdom, and I interpreted them for myself in this manner: I must actively take care of myself, that my life should be better, and I must not impose the care of myself on other people's shoulders; but if I am going to take care of myself alone, of nothing but my own personal life, it will be useless, ugly, meaningless. This thought ate its way deep into my soul, and I say now with conviction: Hillel's wisdom served as a strong staff on my road, which was neither even nor easy.

I believe that Jewish wisdom is more all-human and universal than any other; and this not only because of its immemorial age, not only because it is the firstborn, but also because of the powerful humaneness that saturates it, because of its high estimate of man.

MAXIM GORKY, 1916.

THE PHARISEES

O F all the strange ironies of history, perhaps the strangest is that 'Pharisee' is current as a term of reproach among the theological descendants of that sect of Nazarenes who, without the martyr spirit of those primitive Puritans, would never have come into existence.

T. H. HUXLEY.

THE Pharisees built up religious individualism and a purely spiritual worship; they deepened the belief in a future life; they championed the cause of the laity against an exclusive priesthood; they made the Scriptures the possession of the people, and in the weekly assemblages of the Synagogue they preached to them the truths and hopes of religion out of the Sacred Books.... The Pharisees consistently strove to bring life more and more under the dominion of religious observance. By carefully formed habits, by the ceremonial of religious observances, religious ideas and sanctions could be impressed upon the people's mind and heart. But the outward was subordinated to the inward.

CANON G. H. BOX, 1911.

PHARISAISM in history has had a hard fate. For there has seldom been for Christians the opportunity to know what Pharisaism really meant, and perhaps still more seldom the desire to use that opportunity. Is then the Christian religion so weak that it must be advocated by blackening the character of its oldest rival?

R. TRAVERS HERFORD, 1912.

THE JEWISH PRAYER BOOK

W HEN we come to view the half-dozen or so great Liturgies of
the world purely as religious documents, and to weigh their
value as devotional classics, the incomparable superiority of the Jewish
convincingly appears. The Jewish Liturgy occupies its pages with the
One Eternal Lord; holds ever true, confident, and direct speech with
Him; exhausts the resources of language in songs of praise, in utte-
rances of loving gratitude, in rejoicing at His nearness, in natural
outpourings of grief for sin; never so much as a dream of intercessors
or of hidings from His blessed punishments; and, withal, such a sweet
sense of the divine accessibility every moment to each sinful, suffering
child of earth. Where shall one find a hymn of universal faith like the
Adon Olam, of mystical beauty like the Hymn of Glory; or services so
solemn, touching, and tender as those appointed for Yom
Kippur? Compare the misery, gloom, and introspection surrounding
other requiem and funeral services, with the chastened, dignified
sobriety of the Hebrew prayer for the dying,[1] and the healthy, cheerful
manliness of the Mourner's Kaddish.

Again, there is most refreshing silence in regard to life-conditions
after death. Neither is there any spiteful condemnation of the followers
of other faiths; the Jew is singularly free from narrow intolerance.

Certainly the Jew has cause to thank God, and the fathers before
him, for the noblest Liturgy the annals of faith can show.

G. E. BIDDLE, 1907.

---

1. Authorized Prayer Book, p. 317.

IN A SYNAGOGUE

DERONDA gave himself up to that strongest effect of chanted liturgies which is independent of detailed verbal meaning. The most powerful movement of feeling with a liturgy is the prayer which seeks for nothing special, but is a yearning to escape from the limitations of our own weakness and an invocation of all Good to enter and abide with us; or else a self-oblivious lifting up of gladness, a 'Gloria in excelsis' that such Good exists; both the yearning and the exultation gathering their utmost force from the sense of communion in a form which has expressed them both for long generations of struggling fellow-men. The Hebrew liturgy, like others, has its transitions of litany, lyric proclamation, dry statement, and blessing; but this evening all were one for Deronda; the chant of the Chazan's or Reader's grand wide-ranging voice with its passage from monotony to sudden cries, the outburst of sweet boys' voices from the little choir, the devotional swaying of men's bodies backwards and forwards, the very common-ness of the building and shabbiness of the scene where a national faith, which had penetrated the thinking of half the world, had moulded the splendid forms of that world's religion, was finding a remote, obscure echo—all were blent for him as one expression of a binding history, tragic and yet glorious.

GEORGE ELIOT, 1876.

THE TORCH OF
JEWISH LEARNING

LEARNING was for two thousand years the sole claim to distinction recognized by Israel. 'The scholar', says the Talmud, 'takes precedence over the king.' Israel remained faithful to this precept throughout all her humiliations. Whenever, in Christian or Moslem lands, a hostile hand closed her schools, the rabbis crossed the seas to reopen their academies in a distant country. Like the legendary Wandering Jew, the flickering torch of Jewish scholarship thus passed from East to West, from North to South, changing every two or three hundred years from one country to another. Whenever a royal edict commanded them to leave, within three months, the country in which their fathers had been buried and their sons had been born, the treasure which the Jews were most anxious to carry away with them was their books. Among all the *autos-da-fé* which the daughter of Zion has had to witness, none has cost her such bitter tears as those flames which, during the Middle Ages, greedily consumed the scrolls of the Talmud.

A. LEROY BEAULIEU, 1893.

---

1. From *Israel Among the Nations* (London: Heinemann).

DURING THE CRUSADES

1

IN the little town Tiberias, on the shore of the Lake of Gennesaret, sat the old Jew Eleazar, with his family, prepared to celebrate the Passover. It was the fourteenth day of the month Nisan of the year 1089.

After the head of the family had washed his hands, he blessed the gifts of God, drank some wine, took some of the bitter herbs, and ate and gave to the others. After that, the second cup of wine was served, and the youngest son of the house asked, according to the sacred custom, 'What is the meaning of this feast?'

The father answered: 'The Lord brought us with a strong hand out of the Egyptian bondage'. Thereafter a blessing was pronounced on the unleavened bread, and they sat down to eat. The old Eleazar spoke of past times, and contrasted them with the present: 'Man born of woman lives but a short time, and is full of trouble; he cometh up like a flower, and is cut down; he fleeth hence like a shadow, and continueth not. A stranger and a sojourner is he upon earth, and therefore he should be always ready for his journey as we are, this holy evening.'

The eldest son, Jacob, who had come home in the evening after a journey, seemed to wish to say something, but did not venture to do so till the fourth and last cup was drunk.

'Now, Jacob', said Eleazar, 'you want to talk. You come from a journey, though somewhat late, and have something new to tell us. Hush! I hear steps in the garden!'

All hurried to the window, for they lived in troublous times; but, as no one was to be seen outside, they sat down again at the table.

'Speak, Jacob', Eleazar said again.

'I come from Antioch, where the Crusaders are besieged by Kerboga, the Emir Mosul. Famine has raged among them, and of three hundred thousand Goyim, only twenty thousand remain.'

'What had they to do here?'

'Now, on the roads, they are talking of a new battle which the Goyim have won, and they believe that the Crusaders will march straight on Jerusalem.'

'Well, they won't come here.'

'They won't find the way, unless there are traitors.'

'The Christians are misguided, and their doctrine is folly. They believe the Messiah has come, although the world is like a hell, and men resemble devils! And it ever gets worse....'

Then the door was flung open, and on the threshold appeared a little man, emaciated as a skeleton, with burning eyes—Peter the Hermit. He was clothed in rags, carried a cross in his hands, and bore a red cross-shaped sign on his shoulder.

'Are you Christians?' he asked.

'No', answered Eleazar, 'we are of Israel.'

'Out with you!—down to the lake and be baptized, or you will die the death!'

Then Eleazar turned to the Hermit, and cried, 'No! I and my house will serve the Lord, as we have done this holy evening according to the law of our fathers. We suffer for our sins, that is true, but you, godless, cursed man, pride not yourself on your power, for you have not yet escaped the judgement of Almighty God.'

The Hermit had gone out to his followers. Those within the house closed the window-shutters and the door.

There was a cry without: 'Fire the house!'

'Let us bless God, and die!' said Eleazar, and none of them hesitated. Eleazar spoke: 'I know that my Redeemer liveth, and that He will stand at the latter day upon the earth. And when I am free from my flesh, I shall see God. Him shall I see and not another, and for that my soul and my heart cry out.'

The mother had taken the youngest son in her arms, as though she wished to protect him against the fire which now seized on the wall.

Then Eleazar began the Song of the Three Children[2] in the fire, and when they came to the words,

'O thank the Lord, for He is good,

And His mercy endureth for ever',

their voices were choked, and they ended their days like the Maccabees.

AUGUST STRINDBERG, 1907.

---

1. From *Historical Miniatures* (London: George Allen & Unwin).
2. A book in the Apocrypha.

THE EXPULSION FROM SPAIN AND PORTUGAL, 1492-1497

1

THE persecution of the Jewish race dates from the very earliest period in which Christianity obtained the direction of the civil powers; and the hatred of the Jews was for many centuries a faithful index of the piety of the Christians.

Insulted, plundered, hated, and despised by all Christian nations, banished from England by Edward I, and from France by Charles VI, they found in the Spanish Moors rulers who were probably not without a special sympathy for a race whose pure monotheism formed a marked contrast to the scarcely disguised polytheism of the Spanish Catholics; and Jewish learning and Jewish genius contributed very largely to that bright but transient civilization which radiated from Toledo and Cordova, and exercised so salutary an influence upon the belief of Europe. But when, in an ill-omened hour, the Cross supplanted the Crescent on the heights of the Alhambra, this solitary refuge was destroyed, the last gleam of tolerance vanished from Spain, and the expulsion of the Jews was determined.

This edict was immediately due to the exertions of Torquemada; but its ultimate cause is to be found in that steadily increasing popular fanaticism which made it impossible for the two races to exist together. In 1390, about a hundred years before the conquest of Granada, the Catholics of Seville being excited by the eloquence of a great preacher, named Hernando Martinez, had attacked the Jews' quarter, and murdered 4,000 Jews, Martinez himself presiding over the massacre. About a year later, and partly through the influence of the same eminent divine, similar scenes took place at Valentia, Cordova, Burgos, Toledo, and Barcelona ... and more than once during the fifteenth century. At last the Moorish war, which had always been regarded as a crusade, was drawing to a close, the religious fervour of the Spanish rose to the highest point, and the Inquisition was established as its expression. Numbers of converted Jews were massacred; others, who had been baptized during past explosions of popular fury, fled to the Moors, in order to practise their rites, and at last, after a desperate resistance, were captured and burnt alive. The clergy exerted all their energies to produce the expulsion of the entire race, and to effect this object all the old calumnies were revived, and two or three miracles invented.

It must be acknowledged that history relates very few measures that produced so vast an amount of calamity. In three short months, all unconverted Jews were obliged, under pain of death, to abandon the Spanish soil. Multitudes, falling into the hands of the pirates, who swarmed around the coast, were plundered of all they possessed and reduced to slavery; multitudes died of famine or of plague, or were murdered or tortured with horrible cruelty by the African savages. About 80,000 took refuge in Portugal, relying on the promise of the king. Spanish priests lashed the Portuguese into fury, and the king was persuaded to issue an edict which threw even that of Isabella into the shade. All the adult Jews were banished from Portugal; but first of all their children below the age of fourteen were taken from them to be educated as Christians. Then, indeed, the cup of bitterness was filled to the brim. The serene fortitude with which the exiled people had borne so many and such grievous calamities gave way, and was replaced by the wildest paroxysms of despair. When at last, childless and broken-hearted, they sought to leave the land, they found that the ships had been purposely detained, and the allotted time, having expired, they were reduced to slavery and baptized by force. A great peal of rejoicing filled the Peninsula, and proclaimed that the triumph of the Spanish priests was complete.

Certainly the heroism of the defenders of every other creed fades into insignificance before this martyr people, who for thirteen centuries confronted all the evils that the fiercest fanaticism could devise, enduring obloquy and spoliation and the violation of the dearest ties, and the infliction of the most hideous sufferings, rather than abandon their faith.

Persecution came to the Jewish nation in its most horrible forms, yet surrounded by every circumstance of petty annoyance that could destroy its grandeur, and it continued for centuries their abiding portion. But above all this the genius of that wonderful people rose supreme. While those around them were grovelling in the darkness of besotted ignorance; while juggling miracles and lying relics were the themes on which almost all Europe was expatiating; while the intellect of Christendom, enthralled by countless superstitions, had sunk into a deadly torpor, in which all love of inquiry and all search for truth were abandoned, the Jews were still pursuing the path of knowledge, amassing learning, and stimulating progress with the same unflinching constancy that they manifested in their faith. They were the most skilful physicians, the ablest financiers, and among the most profound philosophers.

W. E. H. LECKY, 1865.

---

1. From *History of Rationalism in Europe* (London: Longmans, Green & Co.).

A PROTEST AGAINST THE AUTO-DA-FÉ OF SEPTEMBER 20, 1761, LISBON

W HAT was their crime? Only that they were born. They were born Israelites, they celebrated Pesach; that is the only reason that the Portuguese burnt them. Would you believe that while the flames were consuming these innocent victims, the inquisitors and the other savages were chanting *our* prayers? These pitiless monsters were invoking the God of mercy and kindness, the God of pardon, while committing the most atrocious and barbarous crime, while acting in a way which demons in their rage would not use against their brother demons. Your madness goes so far as to say that we are scattered because our fathers condemned to death him whom you worship. O ye pious tigers, ye fanatical panthers, who despise your sect so much that you have no better way of supporting it than by executioners, cannot you see that it was only the Romans who condemned him? We had not, at that time, the right to inflict death; we were governed by Quirinus, Varus, Pilate. No crucifixion was practised among us. Not a trace of that form of punishment is to be found. Cease, therefore, to punish a whole nation for an event for which it cannot be responsible. Would it be just to go and burn the Pope and all the Monsignori at Rome to-day because the first Romans ravished the Sabines and pillaged the Samnites?

O God, who hast created us all, who desirest not the misfortune of

Thy creatures, God, Father of all, God of mercy, accomplish Thou that there be no longer on this globe, on this least of all the worlds, either fanatics or persecutors. Amen.

F. M. A. VOLTAIRE, *in 'Sermon du Rabin Akib'.*

THE BIBLE IN
ELIZABETHAN ENGLAND

1

NO greater moral change ever passed over a nation than passed over England during the years of the reign of Elizabeth. England became the people of a book, and that book was the Bible. It was read in churches, and it was read at home, and everywhere its words, as they fell on ears which custom had not deadened to their force and beauty, kindled a startling enthusiasm. As a mere literary monument, the English Version of the Bible remains the noblest example of the English tongue, while its perpetual use made it from the instant of its appearance the standard of our language. But far greater than its effect on literature was the effect of the Bible on the character of the people at large. Elizabeth might silence or tune the pulpits, but it was impossible for her to silence or tune the great preachers of justice, and mercy, and truth, who spoke from the Book which the Lord again opened to the people. The effect of the Bible in this way was simply amazing. The whole temper of the nation was changed. A new conception of life and of man superseded the old. A new moral and religious impulse spread through every class.

J. R. GREEN, 1874.

1. From *A Short History of the English People* (London: Macmillan & Co.).

FOR THE EMANCIPATION
OF THE JEWS

I N the infancy of civilization, when our island was as savage as
New Guinea, when letters and arts were still unknown to Athens,
when scarcely a thatched hut stood on what was afterwards the site of
Rome, this contemned people had their fenced cities and cedar palaces,
their splendid Temple, their fleets of merchant ships, their schools of
sacred learning, their great statesmen and soldiers, their natural philosophers, their historians, and their poets. What nation ever contended
more manfully against overwhelming odds for its independence and
religion? What nation ever, in its last agonies, gave such signal proofs
of what may be accomplished by a brave despair? And if, in the course
of many centuries, the oppressed descendants of warriors and sages
have degenerated from the qualities of their fathers ... shall we consider
this as a matter of reproach to them? Shall we not rather consider it as
matter of shame and remorse to ourselves? Let us do justice to them.
Let us open to them the door of the House of Commons. Let us open to
them every career in which ability and energy can be displayed. Till we
have done this, let us not presume to say that there is no genius among
the countrymen of Isaiah, no heroism among the descendants of the
Maccabees.
LORD MACAULAY, 1833.

IGNORANCE OF JUDAISM

H E had been roused to the consciousness of knowing hardly anything about modern Judaism or the inner Jewish history. The Chosen People have been commonly treated as a people chosen for the sake of somebody else, and their thinking as something (no matter exactly what) that ought to have been entirely otherwise; and Deronda, like his neighbours, had regarded Judaism as a sort of eccentric fossilized form which an accomplished man might dispense with studying, and leave to specialists. But there had flashed on him the hitherto neglected reality that Judaism was something still throbbing in human lives, still making for them the only conceivable vesture of the world.
GEORGE ELIOT, 1876, *in 'Daniel Deronda'*.

MOCK on, mock on, Voltaire, Rousseau!
    Mock on, mock on! 'tis all in vain:
    You throw the sand against the wind,
    And the wind blows it back again.
    And every sand becomes a gem
    Reflected in the beams divine;
    Blown back, they blind the mocking eye,
    But still in Israel's paths they shine.
WILLIAM BLAKE.

THEY ARE OUR ELDERS

NEXT to the selection that has been in operation for centuries, it is, in my opinion, the antiquity and the continuity of their civilization that throws some light upon the Jews as well as upon the place they occupy in our midst. They were here before us; they are our elders. Their children were taught to read from the scrolls of the Torah before our Latin alphabet had reached its final form, long before Cyrillus and Methodius had given writing to the Slavs, and before the Runic characters were known to the Germans of the North. As compared with the Jews, we are young, we are new-comers; in the matter of civilization they are far ahead of us. It was in vain that we locked them up for several hundred years behind the walls of the Ghetto. No sooner were their prison gates unbarred than they easily caught up with us, even on those paths which we had opened up without their aid.

A. LEROY BEAULIEU, 1893.

THE JEWISH CEMETERY
AT NEWPORT

HOW strange it seems! These Hebrews in their graves,
  Close by the street of this fair seaport town,
Silent beside the never-silent waves,
At rest in all this moving up and down.
How came they here? What burst of Christian hate,
What persecution, merciless and blind,
Drove o'er the sea—that desert desolate—
These Ishmaels and Hagars of mankind?
Pride and humiliation hand in hand
Walked with them through the world where'er they went;
Trampled and beaten were they as the sand,
And yet unshaken as the continent.
For in the background figures vague and vast
Of patriarchs and prophets rose sublime,
And all the great traditions of the Past
They saw reflected in the coming time.
And thus forever with reverted look
The mystic volume of the world they read,
Spelling it backward, like a Hebrew book,
Till life became a Legend of the Dead.
H. W. LONGFELLOW, 1858.

THE JEW AS A CITIZEN

I AM glad to be able to say that while the Jews of the United States have remained loyal to their faith and their race traditions, they are engaged in generous rivalry with their fellow-citizens of other denominations in advancing the interests of our common country. This is true, not only of the descendants of the early settlers and those of American birth, but of a great and constantly increasing proportion of those who have come to our shores within the last twenty-five years as refugees reduced to the direst straits of penury and misery. In a few years, men and women hitherto utterly unaccustomed to any of the privileges of citizenship have moved mightily upward toward the standard of loyal, self-respecting American citizenship; of that citizenship which not merely insists upon its rights, but also eagerly recognizes its duty to do its full share in the material, social, and moral advancement of the nation.

THEODORE ROOSEVELT, *on the 250th anniversary of the Settlement of the Jews in the United States, November, 1905.*

IN THE EAST END OF
LONDON

S OME years ago, when I was living in Europe, I went for six
months to reside in the very poorest part of the East End of
London, when I made friends with a poor Jewish woman. She took me
into the tiny one-roomed tenement where she and her husband and
their children lived on the few shillings a week they earned by their
joint labour. Though it had all the misery and confinement which
extreme poverty means in a great city, I had yet often a curious feeling
that it was a *home*. With however much difficulty, a few pence would
be saved to celebrate, if it were but in a pitiful little way, the festivals
of their people; though it were by starving themselves, the parents
would lay by something for the education of their children or to
procure them some little extra comfort. And the conclusion was forced
on me that, taking the very poorest class of Jew and comparing him
with an exactly analogous class of non-Jews earning the same wages
and living in the same locality, the life of the Jew was, on the whole,
more mentally healthful, more human, and had in it an element of hope
that was often wanting in that of others. I felt that these people needed
but a little space, a little chance, to develop into some far higher form.
The material was there.

Therefore I would welcome the exiled Russian Jew to South
Africa, not merely with pity, but with a feeling of pride that any

member of that great, much-suffering people, to whom the world owes so great a debt, should find a refuge and a home among us.

OLIVE SCHREINER, 1906.

THE RUSSIAN AGONY

I. THE BEGINNINGS

IN 1563 Ivan the Terrible conquered Polotzk, and for the first time the Russian Government was confronted by the fact of the existence of the Jewish nationality. The Czar's advisers were somewhat perplexed, and asked him what to do with these newly acquired subjects. Ivan the Terrible answered unhesitatingly: 'Baptize them or drown them in the river'. They were drowned.

P. MILYUKOV, 1916.

II. IN THE NINETEENTH CENTURY[1]

FEW facts in the nineteenth century have been so well calculated to disenchant the believers in perpetual progress with their creed as the anti-Semite movement, which in a few years has swept like an angry wave over the greater part of Europe.

The recent movement for proscribing, under pretence of preventing cruelty to animals, the mode of killing animals for food which is enjoined in the Jewish ritual, is certainly at least as much due to dislike to the Jews as to consideration for cattle. It appears to have arisen among the German anti-Semites, especially in Saxony....

219

The Russian persecution stands in some degree apart from the other forms of the anti-Semite movement, both on account of its unparalleled magnitude and ferocity, and also because it is the direct act of a Government deliberately, systematically, remorselessly seeking to reduce to utter misery millions of its own subjects.

An evil chance had placed upon the throne an absolute ruler who combined with much private virtue and very limited faculties all the genuine fanaticism of the great persecutors of the past, and who found a new Torquemada at his side. He reigned over an administration which is among the most despotic, and probably, without exception, the most corrupt and the most cruel in Europe.

W. E. H. LECKY, 1896.

III. IN THE TWENTIETH CENTURY

TO lock people like wild beasts in a cage, to surround them with disgraceful laws, as in an immense circus, for the sole revolting purpose to let loose the murderous mob upon them whenever practicable for St. Petersburg—terrible, terrible!

Anti-Semitism is a mad passion, akin to the lowest perversities of diseased human nature. It is the will to hate.

The Emperor Hadrian was an honest anti-Semite. One day, the Talmud records, on his journey in the East, a Jew passed the Imperial train and saluted the Emperor. He was beside himself with rage. 'You, a Jew, dare to greet the Emperor! You shall pay for this with your life.' In the course of the same day another Jew passed him, and, warned by example, he did not greet Hadrian. 'You, a Jew, dare to pass the Emperor without a greeting!' he angrily exclaimed. 'You have forfeited your life.' To his astonished courtiers he replied: 'I hate the Jews. Whatever they do, I find intolerable. I therefore make use of any pretext to destroy them.'

So are all anti-Semites.

LEO TOLSTOY, 1904.

IV. THE MORAL

THE study of the history of Europe during the past centuries teaches us one uniform lesson: *That the nations which have received and in any way dealt fairly and mercifully with the Jew have prospered; and that the nations that have tortured and oppressed him have written out their own curse.*
OLIVE SCHREINER, 1906.

----

1. From *Democracy and Liberty* (London: Longmans, Green & Co.).

THE BLOOD LIBEL

BRITISH PROTEST, 1912

WE desire to associate ourselves with the protests signed in Russia, France, and Germany by leading Christian Theologians, Men of Letters, Scientists, Politicians, and others against the attempt made in the City of Kieff to revive the hideous charge of Ritual Murder—known as the 'Blood Accusation'—against Judaism and the Jewish People.

The question is one of humanity, civilization, and truth. The 'blood accusation' is a relic of the days of witchcraft and 'black magic', a cruel and utterly baseless libel on Judaism, an insult to Western culture, and a dishonour to the Churches in whose name it has been falsely formulated by ignorant fanatics. Religious minorities other than the Jews, such as the early Christians, the Quakers, and Christian Missionaries in China, have been victimized by it. It has been denounced by the best men of all ages and creeds. The Popes, the founders of the Reformation, the Khalif of Islam, statesmen of every country, together with all the great seats of learning in Europe, have publicly repudiated it.

Signed by:—
The ARCHBISHOPS *of* CANTERBURY, YORK, ARMAGH; *the*

CARDINAL ARCHBISHOP *of* WESTMINSTER, *and the* HEADS *of all other* CHRISTIAN DENOMINATIONS.

The BISHOPS *of* LONDON, OXFORD, WORCESTER, WINCHESTER, BIRMINGHAM, GLOUCESTER, LIVERPOOL, MANCHESTER, &c.; *the* DEANS *of* WESTMINSTER, CANTERBURY, NORWICH, RIPON, &c.

The DUKES *of* NORFOLK *and* NORTHUMBERLAND, *and the* EARLS *of* ROSEBERY, SELBORNE, *and* CROMER; LORDS MILNER *and* RAYLEIGH; A. J. BALFOUR, SIR EDWARD CARSON, GEN. N. G. LYTTELTON, &c.

FREDERIC HARRISON, A. V. DICEY, SIR WILLIAM OSLER, SIR FRANCIS DARWIN, SIR WILLIAM RAMSAY; JAMES A. H. MURRAY, NORMAN LOCKYER, J. G. FRAZER, &c.

SIR OLIVER LODGE, *the* PRINCIPALS *of eleven* OXFORD COLLEGES; *the* MASTERS *of seven* CAMBRIDGE COLLEGES, S. R. DRIVER, F. C. BURKITT, A. E. COWLEY, W. SANDAY, H. B. SWETE, ESTLIN CARPENTER, A. E. GARVIE, A. C. HEADLAM, KIRSOPP LAKE, &c.

JUSTICES EVE, WARRINGTON, *and* VAUGHAN WILLIAMS.

A. C. DOYLE, THOS. HARDY, ANTHONY HOPE, A. QUILLER-COUCH, G. B. SHAW, H. G. WELLS, &c.

The EDITORS *of the Edinburgh, Quarterly, Fortnightly, Hibbert, Quest, Spectator, Nation, Daily Telegraph, Manchester Guardian, Daily Chronicle, Daily News, Pall Mall Gazette, &c., &c.*

JEWISH NATIONALISM

W HEN it is rational to say, 'I know not my father or my mother, let my children be aliens to me that no prayer of mine may touch them', then it will be rational for the Jew to say, 'I will not cherish the prophetic consciousness of our nationality—let the Hebrew cease to be, and let all his memorials be antiquarian trifles, dead as the wall paintings of a conjectured race'.

The divine principle of our race is action, choice, resolved memory. Let us help to will our own better future and the better future of the world—not renounce our higher gift and say, 'Let us be as if we were not among the populations'; but choose our full heritage, claim the brotherhood of our nation, and carry into it a new brotherhood with the nations of the Gentiles. The vision is there; it will be fulfilled.

GEORGE ELIOT, 1876, *in 'Daniel Deronda'*.

No British Jew would be less British because he looked upon the cradle of his race with pride, and at the religious centre of his faith with happiness and reverence.

SIR MARK SYKES, 1918.

A JEWISH
NATIONAL HOME

FOREIGN OFFICE, *November 2, 1917.*

D EAR LORD ROTHSCHILD,
        I have much pleasure in conveying to you, on behalf of His Majesty's Government, the following declaration of sympathy with Jewish Zionist aspirations which has been submitted to, and approved by, the Cabinet:—

'His Majesty's Government view with favour the establishment in Palestine of a national home for the Jewish people, and will use their best endeavours to facilitate the achievement of this object, it being clearly understood that nothing shall be done which may prejudice the civil and religious rights of existing non-Jewish communities in Palestine, or the rights and political status enjoyed by Jews in any other country.'

Yours sincerely,
ARTHUR JAMES BALFOUR.

ISRAEL'S PRESERVATION

THE destruction of the Holy City, the ruin of the House of God, the dispersion of the Chosen People into all the kingdoms of the earth, and their continued existence as a nation, notwithstanding every attempt to exterminate them or to compel them to forsake those ordinances which distinguish them to this very day from all other nations, is emphatically one of the strongest evidences we can have of the truth of the Bible. Jerusalem was indeed once a great city, and the Temple magnifical; but the Jews themselves were greater than either; hence, while the two former have been given over to spoliation, the latter have been wonderfully, miraculously preserved. The annals of the world do not contain anything so remarkable in human experience, so greatly surpassing human power and human prescience. Exiled and dispersed, reviled and persecuted, oppressed and suffering, often denied the commonest rights of humanity, and still more often made the victim of ruthless fanaticism and bigoted prejudice, the Jews are divinely preserved for a purpose worthy of a God!

ST. JEROME, 4th cent.

ISRAEL AND THE NATIONS

1

THE Jew has made a marvellous fight in this world, in all the ages; and has done it with his hands tied behind him. The Egyptian, the Babylonian, and the Persian rose, filled the planet with sound and splendour, then faded to dream-stuff and passed away; the Greek and the Roman followed, and made a vast noise, and they are gone; other peoples have sprung up and held their torch high for a time, but it burned out, and they sit in twilight now, or have vanished. The Jew saw them all, beat them all, and is now what he always was, exhibiting no decadence, no infirmities of age, no weakening of his parts, no slowing of his energies, no dulling of his alert and aggressive mind.

MARK TWAIN, 1898.

1. From *The Man that Corrupted Hadleyburg* (London: Chatto & Windus).

THE VOICE OF PRAYER (THE JEWISH YEAR)

HOW precious is Thy loving-kindness, O God, and the children of men take refuge under the shadow of Thy wings. For with Thee is the fountain of life; in Thy light do we see light.

PSALM 36. 8, 10.

ON PRAYER AND PRAISE

T HERE is an old story, invented by the sages and handed down by memory from age to age. They say, when God had finished the world, He asked one of the angels if aught were wanting on land or on sea, in air or in heaven. The angel answered that all was perfect; one thing only he desired—speech, to praise God's works, or recount them, which would be their praise. And the Father approved the angel's words, and not long afterwards appeared the race, gifted with the muses and with song. This is the ancient story, and in consonance with its spirit I say: 'It is God's peculiar work to benefit, and His creatures' work to give Him thanks'.

PHILO JUDAEUS, 1st cent.

THERE are halls in the heavens above that open but to the voice of song.

ZOHAR.

ON MORNING SERVICE

L ET man strengthen himself like a lion and arise in the early morn to render service to his Creator; as David said, 'I will awake the dawn' (Psalm 57. 9).

COMMENTARY: *Strengthen himself.*—The root-idea of such strengthening is to prepare himself to resist temptations and evil desires which during this day may assail him: as it is said, 'Who is strong? He that subdues his passions.' *Like a lion.*—As a lion is the most fearless of animals, so shall he likewise, in the performance of his duties, fear nothing, but rely firmly on his God.

GLOSS: 'I have set the Lord always before me' (Psalm 16. 8): This is a leading principle in Religion, and in the upward strivings of the righteous who walk ever in the presence of God. For a man's mode of life, his demeanour and his deeds, his speech and his movements, when alone in the house or in the intimate circle of his family and friends, are unlike those which he would exhibit when in the presence of a great king. And how much more considered will his demeanour be, if he reflect that there stands over him the King of kings, the Holy One, blessed be He, whose glory fills the whole earth, watching his conduct and surveying his deeds; even as it is written: 'Can any hide himself in secret places that I shall not see him?' saith the Lord (Jeremiah 23. 24). Such contemplation must perforce imbue him with a true sense of reverence and humility, prompted by a feeling of unworthiness, before the Holy Name; and he will be heedless of whoever may mock at him because of his devotions.

SHULCHAN ARUCH, 1, § 1. (*Trans. A. Feldman.*)

AT THE DAWN I SEEK THEE

שַׁחַר אֲבַקֶּשְׁךָ,

AT the dawn I seek Thee,
 Refuge, Rock sublime;
Set my prayer before Thee in the morning,
And my prayer at eventime.
I before Thy greatness
Stand and am afraid:
All my secret thoughts Thine eye beholdeth
Deep within my bosom laid.
And, withal, what is it
Heart and tongue can do?
What is this my strength, and what is even
This, the spirit in me, too?
But, indeed, man's singing
May seem good to Thee;
So I praise Thee, singing, while there dwelleth
Yet the breath of God in me.
SOLOMON IBN GABIROL, 1050. (*Trans. Nina Salaman.*)

MORNING PRAYERS

M AY it be Thy will, O God, that I walk in Thy law, and cleave to
Thy commandments. Lead me not into sin or temptation or
contempt. Let not evil desire rule over me. Bend my will to Thine.
Keep me from sinful men and worthless companions. Help me to cling
to the good, and give me grace in Thy sight and in the sight of those
about me. Amen.

DAILY PRAYER BOOK.

O GOD, I stand before Thee, knowing all my deficiencies, and overw-
helmed by Thy greatness and majesty. But Thou hast commanded me
to pray to Thee, and hast suffered me to offer homage to Thine exalted
Name according to the measure of my knowledge, and to lay my
supplication before Thee. Thou knowest best what is for my good. If
I recite my wants, it is not to remind Thee of them, but only so that
I may understand better how great is my dependence upon Thee. If,
then, I ask Thee for the things that make not for my well-being, it is
because I am ignorant; Thy choice is better than mine, and I submit
myself to Thine unalterable decrees and Thy supreme direction.
'O Lord, my heart is not haughty, nor mine eyes lofty; neither do
I exercise myself in great matters, or in things too wonderful for me.

Surely I have stilled and quieted my soul; like a child with his mother, my soul is with me like a weaned child' (Psalm 131).

BACHYA IBN PAKUDAH, 1040.

ADON OLAM

I

THE charm of the Adon Olam consists in the subtle manner in which Jewish dogmatics are associated with the simplest spiritual thoughts. In the first four lines we have a picture of God, the eternal Lord, existing before the creation of the world, existing still when the world shall cease to be. Between the eternal past and the eternal future comes the world of time. This is purely Jewish dogmatics. Aristotle held that the world was eternal; Judaism, that it was created. It is God alone who is eternal. Further, Judaism conceives of God as Something apart from, outside of, His world. He transcends man and the universe. Yet God is also immanent; He dwells within the human soul as well as within the world. God is not one with man, but akin to man; He is high above the world, yet nigh unto them that call upon Him. The God who exists for ever is proclaimed King when men acknowledge His Kingship and show Him the allegiance of worship and obedience. The God who stands high above creation is the One into whose hand man commits himself without fear. The Majestic King is also the Redeemer. The transcendent God is a Refuge in man's distress. He does not merely raise a banner, He is the Banner; He does not only hold out the cup of salvation, He is the consummate Cup.

I. ABRAHAMS, 1906.

II

BEFORE the glorious orbs of light
    Had shed one blissful ray,
    In awful power, the Lord of might
    Reign'd in eternal day.
    At His creative, holy word
    The voice of nature spoke,
    Unnumber'd worlds with one accord
    To living joys awoke.
    Then was proclaim'd the mighty King
    In majesty on high!
    Then did the holy creatures sing
    His praises through the sky.
    All-merciful in strength He reigns
    Immutable! supreme!
    His hand the universe sustains,
    He only can redeem.
    Almighty, powerful and just!
    Thou art my God, my Friend,
    My rock, my refuge and my trust,
    On Thee my hopes depend.
    O! be my guardian whilst I sleep,
    For Thou didst lend me breath:
    And when I wake, my spirit keep,
    And save my soul in death.
    D. N. CARVALHO, 1830.

---

1. Authorized Prayer Book, p. 3.

ADON OLAM AND
MODERN SCIENCE

A LONE of all religious and philosophic conceptions of man, the faith which binds together the Jews has not been harmed by the advance of research, but, on the contrary, has been vindicated in its profoundest tenets. Slowly and by degrees Science is being brought to recognize in the universe the existence of One Power, which is of no beginning and no end; which has existed before all things were formed, and will remain in its integrity when all is gone; the Source and Origin of all, in Itself beyond any conception or image that man can form and set up before his eye or mind; whereas all things perceivable as matter and force are subjected to his inquiry and designs. This sum total of the scientific discoveries of all lands and times is an approach of the world's thought to our Adon Olam, the sublime chant, by means of which the Jew has wrought and will further work the most momentous changes in the world.

W. M. HAFFKINE, 1916.

THE SHEMA

שְׁמַ_ע יִ_שְׂ_רָ_אֵ_ל

'HEAR, O Israel, the Lord is our God, the Lord is one.' That is at once the quintessential embodiment of all our philosophy, as well as chief among Israel's contributions to the everlasting truths of religion. The first prayer of innocent child-lips, the last confession of the dying, the Shema has been the watchword and the rallying-cry of a hundred generations in Israel. By it were they welded into one Brotherhood to do the will of their Father who is in heaven. The reading of the Shema has—in rabbinic phrase—clothed Israel with invincible lion-strength, and endowed him with the double-edged sword of the spirit against the unutterable terrors of his long night of exile.

J. H. HERTZ, 1912.

WHEN men in prayer declare the Unity of the Holy Name in love and reverence, the walls of earth's darkness are cleft in twain, and the Face of the Heavenly King is revealed, lighting up the universe.

ZOHAR.

'THE SOUL THOU HAST
GIVEN ME IS PURE'

אֱלֹהַי נְשָׁמָה

NEXT to God's unity, the most essential and characteristic doctrine of Judaism is that concerning God's relation to man. Heathenism degraded man by making him kneel before brutes and the works of his hand: Judaism declared man to be made in the image of God, the crown and culmination of God's creation, the appointed ruler of the earth. In him, as the end of Creation, the earthly and the divine are singularly blended.

Judaism rejects the idea of an inherent impurity in the flesh or in matter as opposed to the spirit. Nor does Judaism accept the doctrine of Original Sin. In the words of the daily morning prayer, 'The soul that Thou hast given me is pure, Thou hast created it, Thou hast fashioned it, and Thou hast breathed it into me, and Thou preservest it within me, and at the appointed time Thou wilt take it from me to return it within me in the future'.

K. KOHLER, 1904, *in Jewish Encyclopedia*.

THE 'MERIT OF THE FATHERS'

ז ָכ ּו ׁת ֲא ָב ֹו ׁת

JUDAISM insists that man has an inborn impulse to virtue ('Original Virtue') which can overcome all temptation to sin; an impulse immeasurably strengthened through the merit of the fathers (*Zechuth Aboth*) which is accounted unto their children as righteousness. That man is best able to advance on the road to moral perfection who starts with the accumulated spiritual heritage of righteous ancestors.

S. LEVY, 1905.

THE old Jewish doctrine of the 'merit of the fathers' has a counterpart —the idea that the righteousness of the living child favourably affects the fate of the dead father. This might be called the doctrine of the 'merit of the children'. In this way the living and the dead hold converse. The real message of the dead is—their virtue. The real response of the living is again—their virtue. Thus is a bridge built over the chasm of the tomb. Thus do the hearts of fathers and children beat in eternal unison.

I. ABRAHAMS, 1919.

THE KADDISH

ITS origin is mysterious; angels are said to have brought it down from heaven and taught it to men. About this prayer the tenderest threads of filial feeling and human recollection are entwined; for it is the prayer of the orphans! When the father or the mother dies, the surviving sons are to recite it twice daily, morning and evening, throughout the year of mourning, and then also on each recurring anniversary of the death—on the *Yahrzeit*.

It possesses wonderful power. Truly, if there is any bond strong and indissoluble enough to chain heaven to earth, it is this prayer. It keeps the living together, and forms the bridge to the mysterious realm of the dead. One might almost say that this prayer is the watchman and the guardian of the people by whom alone it is uttered; therein lies the warrant of its continuance. Can a people disappear and be annihilated so long as a child remembers its parents? It may sound strange: in the midst of the wildest dissipation has this prayer recalled to his better self many a dissolute character, so that he has bethought himself and for a time at least purified himself by honouring the memory of his parents.

Because this prayer is a resurrection in the spirit of the perishable in man, because it does not acknowledge death, because it permits the blossom which, withered, has fallen from the tree of mankind to flower and develop again in the human heart, therefore it possesses sanctifying power. To know that when thou diest, the earth falling on thy head will not cover thee entirely; to know that there remain behind, those who, wherever they may be on this wide earth, whether they may be poor or rich, will send this prayer after thee; to know that thou leavest them no house, no estate, no field by which they must remember thee, and that yet they will cherish thy memory as their dearest inheritance—what more satisfying knowledge canst thou ever hope for? And such is the knowledge bequeathed to us all by the Kaddish.

L. KOMPERT.

THE souls of the righteous are in the hand of God, and no torment shall touch them. They are in peace. Their hope is full of immortality.

WISDOM OF SOLOMON 3. 1, 3, 4.

AND they that be wise shall shine as the brightness of the firmament; and they that turn many to righteousness as the stars for ever and ever.

DANIEL 12. 3.

THE HOLINESS OF HOME

I T is impossible to describe to those who have not experienced it, the feeling of holy joy which is diffused throughout the humblest Hebrew home by the solemn repetition of acts which in themselves may be regarded as mere customs, without vital connexion with the souls of men. And the particular institution in which it is embodied most characteristically is that of the Sabbath. I do not know how it has come about that a 'Judaic Sabbath' means a day of austere gloom. As a matter of fact, it is the one bright spot in the Jewish life. All is joy and good-humour in the Jewish home on the Friday night, when Sabbath 'comes in'. I would attribute a good deal of the difference between the Jewish and the Christian Sabbath to the seemingly mechanical difference that the former begins and ends at an hour when its advent or exit can be solemnized by ceremonial. It is, indeed, to the Sabbath primarily, and the other home ceremonials which embody the Hebraic conception of the Holiness of the Home, that we can trace the remarkable persistence of the Jewish race through the ages.
JOSEPH JACOBS, 1889.

THE patriarchal feeling still lingers about his hearth. A man, however fallen, who loves his home, is not wholly lost. The trumpet of Sinai still sounds in the Hebrew ear.   BENJAMIN DISRAELI.

245

KINDLING THE SABBATH LIGHT

FROM memory's spring flows a vision to-night,
    My mother is kindling and blessing the light;
The light of Queen Sabbath, the heavenly flame,
That one day in seven quells hunger and shame.
My mother is praying and screening her face,
Too bashful to gaze at the Sabbath light's grace.
She murmurs devoutly, 'Almighty, be blessed,
For sending Thy angel of joy and of rest.
'And may as the candles of Sabbath divine
The eyes of my son in Thy Law ever shine.'
Of childhood, fair childhood, the years are long fled:
Youth's candles are quenched, and my mother is dead.
And yet ev'ry Friday, when twilight arrives,
The face of my mother within me revives;
A prayer on her lips, 'O Almighty, be blessed,
For sending us Sabbath, the angel of rest.'
And some hidden feeling I cannot control
A Sabbath light kindles deep, deep in my soul.
P. M. RASKIN.

LECHA DODI

לְ כָ ה דו ֹד ִי

C OME, my beloved, with chorusing praise,
   Welcome the Sabbath Bride, Queen of the days.
Sabbath, to welcome thee, joyous we haste;
Fountain of blessing from ever thou wast,
First in God's planning, though fashioned the last—
Crown of His handiwork, chiefest of days.
City of holiness, filled are the years;
Up from thine overthrow! Forth from thy fears!
Long hast thou dwelt in the valley of tears,
Now shall God's tenderness shepherd thy ways.
Wake and bestir thee, for come is thy light!
Up! With thy shining the world shall be bright.
Sing! For thy Lord is revealed in His might—
Thine is the splendour His glory displays!
SOLOMON HALEVI ALKABETZ, 16th cent. (*Trans. S. Solis-Cohen.*)

FAR more than Israel has kept the Sabbath, it is the Sabbath that has kept Israel.   ACHAD HA'AM, 1898.

SABBATH PRAYER

BLESSED be the name of the Sovereign of the universe. Blessed be Thy crown and Thy abiding-place. Let Thy favour rest with Thy people Israel for ever: show them the redemption of Thy right hand in Thy holy temple. Vouchsafe unto us the benign gift of Thy light, and in mercy accept our supplications. May it be Thy will to prolong our life in well-being. Let me also be numbered among the righteous, so that Thou mayest be merciful unto me, and have me in Thy keeping, with all that belong to me and to Thy people Israel. Thou art He that feedeth and sustaineth all; Thou art He that ruleth over all; Thou art He that ruleth over kings, for dominion is Thine. I am the servant of the Holy One, blessed be He, before whom and before whose glorious Law I prostrate myself at all times; not in man do I put my trust, nor upon any angel do I rely, but upon the God of Heaven, who is the God of truth, and whose Law is truth, and whose prophets are prophets of truth, and who aboundeth in deeds of goodness and truth. In Him I put my trust, and unto His holy and glorious name I utter praises. May it be Thy will to open my heart unto Thy Law, and to fulfil the wishes of my heart and of the hearts of all Thy people Israel for good, for life, and for peace.

ZOHAR.

THE SABBATH

NOT for us the Sabbath of the quiet streets,
　　Sabbath, peaceful o'er the world outspread,
Felt where every man his neighbour greets,
Heard in hush of many a slowly passing tread.
Not the robe of silence for our holy day:
Noisy run the worker and the player;
Toil and stir and laughter of the way
Surge around the steps that seek a place of prayer.
Silent we, while through the thronging street and mart
Work-day clamour of the city rolls:
Cloistered inly, from the world apart,
Ours it is to bear the Sabbath in our souls.
NINA SALAMAN, 1918.

PRAYER BEFORE THE NEW MOON

MAY it be Thy will, O Lord our God and the God of our fathers, to renew unto us this coming month for good and for blessing. O grant us long life, a life of blessing, of sustenance, of bodily vigour, a life marked by the fear of Heaven and the dread of sin, a life free from shame and reproach; a life in which the desires of our heart shall be fulfilled for good.

May the Holy One, blessed be He, renew it unto us and unto all His people, the house of Israel, for life and peace, for gladness and joy, for salvation and consolation; and let us say, Amen.

DAILY PRAYER BOOK.

THE SEDER

1

FAIR is the twilight,
And fragrant and still:
Little by little
The synagogues fill.
One by one kindle
The night's gleaming eyes;
Candles in windows
And stars in the skies.
Ended in *Shool* is
The service divine;
Seder is started
With legends and wine.
Father is blessing
The night of all nights;
All who are hungry
To feast he invites.
'All who are homeless
Yet masters shall be,
Slaves who are this year—
The next shall be free!'
Children ask 'questions',

And father replies;
Playfully sparkle
The wine and the eyes.
Hymns of redemption
All merrily sing;
Queen is each mother,
Each father a king.
Midnight. The Seder
Is come to an end;
Guardian angels
From heaven descend.
Each one a message
Of liberty brings;
Scattering blessings
Of peace from his wings.
P. M. RASKIN.

---

1. From *A Short History of the English People* (London: Macmillan & Co.).

ISRAEL'S WATCH-NIGHT

לֵיל שִׁמֻּ־וּ־רִים

I SRAEL'S great watch-night dates its origin from the very
Deliverance it was to commemorate through all the coming years.
Ah! With what a delirious impatience did Pharaoh's slaves await the
midnight hour that was to be at once the knell of Egypt's tyranny and
the joy-note that announced their own freedom! God Himself had
singled it out as the time for fulfilling His ancient promise—singled it
out, as the Rabbins tell us in hyperbolical language, from the days of
creation itself. Too long had unrighteousness flourished. Too long had
God seemed to slumber in His Heaven; but now He was to show that
the cry of the oppressed had never failed to reach Him, for accumulated wrongs were to be redressed by a complete and unparalleled deliverance. It was for so signal a vindication of the Divine justice that this
night was reserved. It was as though the Supreme had set His finger
upon this night, in the almanac of Heaven, and declared: This shall
witness the long-deferred triumph of Right over Might; this shall tell
for all time that I am the Lord, that I reign, and that righteousness and
justice are the foundation of My throne, the principles on which I go-
vern My world. This night shall show to all coming generations that it
is only the fool who says in his heart 'There is no God'; that the earthly

despot who pursues his career of cruelty, thinking that he has only his victims' tears to reckon with, is deluding himself to his own ruin.

And is this truth not worth treasuring in these latter days? Often does God seem to hide Himself, to have deserted earth and shut Himself up in Heaven. It is the souls of the meek and the faithful from which humanity's tears are distilled, from which the painful chorus of a world's lament goes up, and seemingly up in vain. But the lesson taught to Pharaoh and to Israel on that awful, that joyous night of deliverance, is still a living lesson; not one jot of its force is abated. God neither slumbers nor sleeps. He watches ever. Not one sigh passes unrecorded in the Heavenly Volume.

MORRIS JOSEPH, 1893.

PASSOVER AND FREEDOM

P ASSOVER is the Festival of Spring. Its human appeal, therefore, is as old as humanity, and as perennial as Spring. But it is as an historical festival,—Israel's birthday—as the annual commemoration of an event which has changed the destinies of mankind, that it proclaims the man-redeeming truth, God is the God of Freedom. Even as in Egypt He espoused the cause of brick-making helots against the mighty royal oppressor, He for ever judgeth the world in righteousness, and the peoples with equity. There is an overruling Providence that exalts righteousness and freedom and humbles the Dominion of iniquity and oppression. This teaching has been as a light unto the nations of the Western world in their weary, age-long warfare for liberty.

J. H. HERTZ, 1918.

THE Passover affirms the great truth that liberty is the inalienable right of every human being. The Feast of Israel's freedom, its celebration is Israel's homage to the great principle of *human freedom*.

MORRIS JOSEPH, 1903.

'ADDIR HU'

G OD of Might,
    God of Right,
Thee we give all glory.
Thine the praise
In our days
As in ages hoary.
When we hear,
Year by year,
Our redemption's story,
Now as erst,
When Thou first
Mad'st the proclamation,
Warning loud
Ev'ry proud,
Ev'ry tyrant nation,
We Thy fame
Still proclaim,
God of our salvation.
G. GOTTHEIL.

WHEN the Egyptian hosts were drowning in the Red Sea, the

angels in heaven were about to break forth in songs of jubilation. But the Holy One, blessed be He, silenced them with the words: 'My creatures are perishing, and ye are ready to sing!'

TALMUD.

THE FEAST OF WEEKS

F OR ever, O Lord,
      Thy word is settled in heaven.
Thy faithfulness is unto all generations:
Thou hast established the earth, and it abideth.
They abide this day according to Thine ordinances;
For all things are Thy servants.
Unless Thy law had been my delight,
I should then have perished in mine affliction.
I have seen an end of all perfection;
But Thy commandment is exceeding broad.
Thy commandments make me wiser than mine enemies;
For they are ever with me.
I have more understanding than all my teachers;
For Thy testimonies are my meditation.
I understand more than the aged,
Because I have kept Thy precepts.
I have refrained my feet from every evil way,
That I might observe Thy word.
I have not turned aside from Thy judgements;
For Thou hast taught me.
PSALM 119. 90-2; 96; 98-102.

A SELF-DENYING GUILD

I S there not something spiritually attractive in the idea of the Jew of this age voluntarily submitting to restrictions on his appetites for the sake of duty—forming one of a religious guild whose special characteristic is self-control? It ought to be the pride of the modern Jew —and every child should be taught to feel it—that his religion demands from him a self-abnegation from which other religionists are absolved; that the price to be paid for the privilege of belonging to the hierarchy of Israel is continuous and conscious self-sacrifice.

The Dietary Laws foster this spirit of self-surrender. Respect for them teaches and helps the Jew, in Rabbinic language, to abase his desires before the will of his Father in Heaven.

MORRIS JOSEPH, 1893.

WITH everlasting love Thou hast loved the house of Israel, Thy people; a Law and commandments, statutes and judgements, hast Thou taught us. Therefore, O Lord our God, when we lie down and when we rise up we will meditate on Thy statutes; yea, we will rejoice in the words of Thy Law and in Thy commandments for ever; for they are our life and the length of our days.

DAILY PRAYER BOOK.

AKDOMUS

אַ_קְ דָ מוּ ת

C OULD we with ink the ocean fill,
  Were every blade of grass a quill,
Were the world of parchment made,
And every man a scribe by trade,
To write the love
Of God above
Would drain that ocean dry;
Nor would the scroll
Contain the whole,
Though stretched from sky to sky!
MEIR BEN ISAAC NEHORAÏ, 1050.

THE BIBLE

I S it a book, a world, a heaven?
    Are those words, or flames, or shining stars,
Or burning torches, or clouds of fire
What is it, I ask ye—the Bible?
Who inspired those infinite truths?
Who spoke through the mouth of the prophet?
Who mapped out the highways of ages,
The glorious lines of the Scriptures?
Who planted the flowers of wisdom
In this sacred soil of the angels?
O dream of eternity—Bible—
O Light that is all and for ever.
MORRIS ROSENFELD, 1918.

THE SEPHER TORAH

1

FOR any community of people to be, and to remain, Jewish, they must be brought up from their tenderest childhood to regard the Sepher Torah as the title-deed of their birthright and pedigree, which they are religiously to hand down unaltered from generation to generation. For is there a Jewish community anywhere, however safely domiciled, which has relinquished the Torah for even one generation and has survived that separation? The Jewish masses, though dispersed to the four winds of the world and mostly destitute of mere shelter—*because tenacious of their creed*, endure, true to themselves and to their past.

The Torah, therefore, is a fountain of life. In it is protection greater than in fortresses. Those who forsake the Torah, bringing it into disrepute and weakening the hold it has on us, are working at the destruction of the brotherhood that cradled and sheltered their fathers and forefathers through all the vicissitudes of the bygone ages, to whom they owe their own life and presence on earth.

W. M. HAFFKINE, 1917.

---

1. *Scroll of the Law.*

RELIGION AND MORALITY

'I AM the Lord thy God'—the pronouncement that forms the introduction to the Decalogue—is rightly regarded as the indispensable basis for all the Commandments, upon whose conscientious fulfilment the well-being of humanity depends. The identification of moral laws with religious precepts, which has been so fully accomplished for the first time in the Law of Moses, gives to the Bible its exceptional importance as a regulator of the conduct of men and of nations. Those who are convinced that by wronging their fellow-men, or transgressing any of the established laws, they violate a command that comes from God, and defy the will of their Maker as expressed in His law, are much less liable to wrongdoing than those who create their own ethical theories and set up their own standards of right and wrong, relying upon their conscience and sense of honour as infallible guides. To some it seems a kind of humiliation if a super-human authority is pointed to as the indispensable guide of human conduct. But man ought never to have assumed such pride as to feel humiliated by the idea of his imperfection and his need of guidance and restraint. History does not justify this pride.
SALIS DAICHES, 1910.

SYMBOLS AND
CEREMONIES

Y OU have heard that in Egypt the waters of the Nile overflowing
its banks, take the place of rain; and that these fructifying waters
are led by various channels into the remote fields to irrigate them.
Now, the Nile with its precious floods would be of no benefit to the
fields without these channels. Thus it is with the Torah and the *Mitz-voth*[1]. The Torah is the mighty stream of spirituality flowing since
ancient times through Israel. It would have caused no useful fruits to
grow, and would have produced no spiritual progress, no moral advancement, had the Mitzvah not been there to lead its divine floods into
the houses, the hearts, and the minds of the individual members of the
people, by connecting practical life in all its variety and its activities
with the spiritual truths of religion.

It is the greatest mistake, based on an entire misunderstanding of
human nature, to assume that men are capable of living in a world of
ideas only, and can dispense with symbols that should embody these
ideas and give them tangibility and visible form. Only the Mitzvah is
the ladder connecting heaven and earth. The Tefillin, containing among
others the commandment: 'Thou shalt love the Lord thy God with all
thine heart, with all thy soul, and with all thy might', are laid on the
head, the seat of thought, and on the arm, the instrument of action,
opposite to the heart, the seat of feeling; thus teaching that all our
thoughts, feelings, and actions must conform to the will of God. This

Mitzvah, performed daily, has contributed more effectively to preserve and to further the morality of our people than have all the learned books on ethics written by our religious philosophers.

M. JUNG, 1917.

---

1. Plural of *Mitzvah*, a ritual precept or ceremonial law. *Mitzvah* also means 'a good deed'.

CUSTOM IN RELIGION

R ELIGION, they say, is only custom. I might agree with this if the 'only' were left out. Customs are the flowers of civilization. You can tell a man's education, yea, even much of his character, by his habits. Morality, ethics, are words derived from roots denoting that which is acknowledged and adopted by the people as right and proper. Manners and usages are the silent compact, the unwritten law which preserve the proprieties of civilized society.

Religion will not come to our aid the moment we call for her; she must be loved and cherished at all times if she is to prove our true friend in need. Much of the present indifference of our young people is directly traceable to the absence of all religious observances in their homes. Piety is the fruit of religious customs.

G. GOTTHEIL, 1896.

'IN ACCORDANCE WITH THE TIMES'

W AS Judaism ever 'in accordance with the times'? Did Judaism ever correspond with the views of dominant contemporaries? Was it ever convenient to be a Jew or a Jewess?

Was the Judaism of our ancestors in accordance with the times, when compelled by the Egyptians to bend their necks during centuries under the yoke of slavery and to suffer their babes to be buried in the waves of the Nile? Was the Judaism of the Maccabees in accordance with their times, when they resisted to the utmost the introduction of Grecian manners prevailing in their days? When the Temple at Jerusalem was destroyed by the Romans and the sons of Judah were slaughtered, sold in slave markets, cast before wild beasts or scattered through every country then known; when Worldly Wisdom would have taught, 'Now it is certainly impossible for us to remain Jews'—did not the Hillels and the son of Zakkai[1] teach yet more earnestly the holiness of our laws and our customs, and so order and regulate things that not a fibre might be lost from the ancestral sanctuary? Was that Judaism in accordance with the times, for which, during the centuries following the Dispersion, our fathers suffered in all lands, through all the various periods, the most degrading oppression, the most biting contempt, and a thousand-fold death and persecution?

And yet *we* would make it the aim and scope of Judaism to be always 'in accordance with the times'!

267

SAMSON RAPHAEL HIRSCH, 1854. (*Trans. Isaac Leeser.*)

---

1. Johanan ben Zakkai, pupil of Hillel and leader of Israel after the Destruction of Jerusalem (70 C.E.). He rescued Judaism by founding the Academy at Jabneh.

FAITH

W HILE faith and reason are blended in the religion of Israel as perhaps in no other, it is not the second place that must be assigned to faith. From the foot of Sinai there is wafted to us the voice declaring with the most perfect childlike faith, '*All that the Lord hath spoken we will do and we will hear*'. It is not surprising that a people who, in their infancy, could give utterance to an expression of trust so childlike, yet so sublime, should produce a prophet who summed up the whole of Israel's law in the words, '*The just shall live by his faith*'.

SIMEON SINGER, 1906.

ODE TO ZION

צִיּוֹן הֲלֹא תִּשְׁאֲלִי (HYMN FOR THE FAST OF AB)

A RT thou not, Zion, fain
    To send forth greetings from thy sacred rock
Unto thy captive train,
Who greet thee as the remnants of thy flock?
Take Thou on every side,
East, west and south and north, their greetings multiplied.
Sadly he greets thee still,
The prisoner of hope who, day and night,
Sheds ceaseless tears, like dew on Hermon's hill.
Would that they fell upon thy mountain's height!
Harsh is my voice when I bewail thy woes,
But when in fancy's dreams
I see thy freedom, forth its cadence flows,
Sweet as the harps that hung by Babel's streams.
The glory of the Lord will ever be
Thy sole and perfect light;
No need hast thou then, to illumine thee
Of sun by day, or moon and stars by night.
I would that, where God's spirit was of yore
Poured out unto thy holy ones, I might

There too my soul outpour.
Oh, who will lead me on
To seek the spots where, in far distant years,
The angels in their glory dawned upon
Thy messengers and seers!
Oh, who will give me wings
That I may fly away,
And there, at rest from all my wanderings,
The ruins of my heart among thy ruins lay?
I'll bend my face unto thy soil, and hold
Thy stones as special gold.
And when in Hebron I have stood beside
My fathers' tombs, then will I pass in turn
Thy plains and forest wide,
Until I stand on Gilead and discern
Mount Hor and Mount Abarim, 'neath whose crest
Thy luminaries twain, thy guides and beacons rest.
Thy air is life unto my soul, thy grains
Of dust are myrrh, thy streams with honey flow
Naked and barefoot to thy ruined fanes
How gladly would I go!
To where the ark was treasured, and in dim
Recesses dwelt the holy cherubim.
Perfect in beauty, Zion, how in thee
Do love and grace unite!
The souls of thy companions tenderly
Turn unto thee; thy joy was their delight,
And weeping they lament thy ruin now.
In distant exile, for thy sacred height
They long, and towards thy gates in prayer they bow.
Shinar and Pathros! come they near to thee?
Naught are they by thy light and right divine.
To what can be compared the majesty
Of thy anointed line?
To what the singers, seers, and Levites thine?
The rule of idols fails and is cast down;
Thy power eternal is, from age to age thy crown.
The Lord desires thee for His dwelling-place
Eternally, and bless'd

Is he whom God has chosen for the grace
Within thy courts to rest.
Happy is he that watches, drawing near,
Until he sees thy glorious lights arise,
And over whom thy dawn breaks full and clear,
Set in the Orient skies.
But happiest he, who, with exultant eyes,
The bliss of thy redeemed ones shall behold,
And see thy youth renewed as in the days of old.
YEHUDAH HALEVI, 1145. (*Trans. Alice Lucas.*)

THE ETERNAL CITY OF THE ETERNAL PEOPLE

JERUSALEM, the hearth of pure religion, the home of prophecy, the sacred fountain of the word of God, is the very emblem of the deathlessness of the spirit. With its 4,000 years' history it is coeval with the Jew, and is as unique among cities as is Israel among the nations. Like the Jew, this Holy City of Israel—the spiritual capital of humanity that has for ages been the magnetic pole of the love and reverence of mankind—is deathless; fire and sword and all the engines of destruction have been hurled against it in vain. A score of conquerors have held it as their choicest prize; and more than a dozen times has it been utterly destroyed. The Assyrians burnt it and deported its population; the Romans slew a million of its inhabitants, razed it to the ground, passed the ploughshare over it, and strewed its furrows with salt; Hadrian banished its very name from the lips of men, changed it to 'Aelia Capitolina', and prohibited any Jew from entering its precincts on pain of death. Persians and Arabs, Barbarians and Crusaders and Turks, took it and retook it, ravaged it and burnt it; and yet, marvellous to relate, it ever rises from its ashes to renewed life and glory. And now, on the very day that 2,080 years ago Judah Maccabee rescued it from the heathens, the Holy City has passed into British occupation! What a privilege it is to have lived to see such a world-historic event! A new future, with undreamt-of possibilities, opens before this eternal city of the eternal people. But in the future, as in the

273

past, it will proclaim the prophetic teaching of the Maccabean festival: *'Not by might, nor by power, but by My spirit, saith the Lord of Hosts'*.

J. H. HERTZ, *at the Thanksgiving Service for the Taking of Jerusalem by H. M. Forces*, 1917.

ARISE, shine, for thy light is come
    And the glory of the Lord is risen upon thee.
    Lift up thine eyes round about, and see:
    They all are gathered together, and come to thee;
    Thy sons come from far,
    And thy daughters are borne on the side.
    Then thou shalt see and be radiant,
    And thy heart shall throb and be enlarged.
    Whereas thou hast been forsaken and hated,
    So that no man passed through thee,
    I will make thee an eternal excellency,
    A joy of many generations.
    Thy sun shall no more go down,
    Neither shall thy moon withdraw itself,
    For the Lord shall be thine everlasting light,
    And the days of thy mourning shall be ended.
    ISAIAH 60. 1, 4–5, 15, 20.

NEW YEAR

INTO the tomb of ages past
        Another year hath now been cast;
Shall time unheeded take its flight,
Nor leave one ray of higher light
That on man's pilgrimage may shine
And lead his soul to spheres divine?
Ah! which of us, if self-reviewed,
Can boast unfailing rectitude?
Who can declare his wayward will
More prone to righteous deed than ill?
Or, in his retrospect of life,
No traces find of passion's strife?
With firm resolve your bosoms nerve
The God of right alone to serve;
Speech, thought, and act to regulate
By what His perfect laws dictate;
Nor from His holy precepts stray,
By worldly idols lured away.
Peace to the house of Israel:
May joy within it ever dwell!
PENINA MOÏSE, 1838.

WRITTEN AND SEALED

'TO be inscribed in the Book of Life.' This must be understood in a spiritual sense. When a man clings to the love of God, and, putting his trust in His infinite mercy, takes upon himself the yoke of the Kingdom of heaven—he therewith inscribes himself in the Book of Life. Whereas the man, a slave to his passions, who so loses his belief in the all-embracing love of God that he fails to repent and return to his Father in heaven, this despairing of the love of God is equivalent to his being inscribed—God forbid—in the Book of Death.

ISRAEL BAALSHEM, 1700.

IN a higher than their literal sense the words of the liturgy are true. Our destiny—our spiritual destiny—is written down on New Year's Day and sealed on the Day of Atonement. We write it down in the penitence with which we greet the dawn of the year, we seal it with the amendment which we solemnly vow on the Fast of Kippur. The time for penitence is with us; the Fast with its supreme task awaits us. Let our endeavours to see ourselves as we really are, our sorrow for our shortcomings, the unrest of our unshriven soul, prepare us for the final act of atonement. The Day of Atonement shall lead us, with hearts bowed in submission, to the Divine throne; and God will lovingly lift us up, absolved, forgiven, filled with the spirit of faith and loving obedience. We shall begin to live at last, to live before Him, to live the true life which is inspired by the constant thought of His presence.

MORRIS JOSEPH.

THE SHOFAR

THE Scriptural injunction of the Shofar for the New Year's Day has a profound meaning. It says: Awake, ye sleepers, and ponder your deeds; remember your Creator, and go back to Him in penitence. Be not of those that miss realities in their hunt after shadows, and waste their years in seeking after vain things which cannot profit or deliver. Look well to your souls and consider your acts; forsake each of you his evil ways and thoughts, and return to God, so that He may have mercy upon you.

MOSES MAIMONIDES, 1180.

FOR this commandment which I command thee this day, it is not too hard for thee, neither is it far off. It is not in heaven that thou shouldst say: 'Who shall go up for us to heaven, and bring it unto us, and make us to hear it, that we may do it?' Neither is it beyond the sea, that thou shouldst say: 'Who shall go over the sea for us, and bring it unto us, and make us to hear it, that we may do it?' But the word is very nigh unto thee, in thy mouth, and in thy heart, that thou mayest do it.

DEUTERONOMY 30. 11-14.

THE Lord is my light and my salvation; whom shall I fear? The Lord is the stronghold of my life; of whom shall I be afraid?

PSALM 27. 1.

MY KING

E RE time began, ere age to age had thrilled,
　　I waited in His storehouse, as He willed.
He gave me being; but, my years fulfilled,
I shall be summoned back before the King.
Thou gavest me a light my path to guide,
To prove my heart's recesses still untried;
And as I went, Thy voice in warning cried:
'Child! fear thou Him who is thy God and King!'
Erring, I wandered in the wilderness,
In passion's grave nigh sinking, powerless;
Now deeply I repent, in sore distress,
That I kept not the statutes of the King!
Thine is the love, O God, and Thine the grace
That folds the sinner in its mild embrace;
Thine the forgiveness bridging o'er the space
'Twixt man's works and the task set by the King.
Unheeding all my sins, I cling to Thee!
I know that mercy will Thy footstool be;
Before I call, oh! do Thou answer me,
For nothing dare I claim of Thee, my King.
MOSES BEN NACHMAN, 1300. (*Trans. Alice Lucas.*)

THE LORD IS KING, THE LORD WAS KING, THE LORD SHALL BE KING FOR EVER AND EVER

¹

THY people in passionate worship cry
One to another the Lord is King.
In awe of the marvels beneath the sky
Each explains that the Lord was King.
One sound from Thy pastures ascends on high:
The chant that the Lord shall be King for ever.
The Lord is King, the Lord was King, the Lord shall be King for ever and ever.
The universe throbs with Thy pauseless praise,
Chorus eternal, the Lord is King.
Thy glory is cried from the dawn of days,
Worshippers calling the Lord was King.
And ever the Saints who shall witness Thy ways
Shall cry that the Lord shall be King for ever.
The Lord is King, the Lord was King, the Lord shall be King for ever and ever.
ELEAZAR KALIR, 8th cent. (*Trans. I. Zangwill.*)

---

1. From *Service of the Synagogue* (George Routledge & Sons).

IF NOT HIGHER

A ND the Rebbe[1] of Nemirov, every Friday Morning early at Sliches[2]-time, disappeared, melted into thin air! He was not to be found anywhere, either in the synagogue or in the two houses-of-study, or worshipping in some Minyan[3], and most certainly not at home. His door stood open, people went in and out as they pleased—no one ever stole anything from the Rebbe—but there was not a soul in the house.

Where can the Rebbe be?

Where should he be, with the Solemn Days so near, if not in heaven? Jews need a livelihood, peace, health; they wish to be good and pious, and their sins are great, and Satan with his thousand eyes spies out the world from one end to the other, and he sees, and accuses, and tells tales—and who shall help if not the Rebbe? So thought the people.

Once, however, there came a Lithuanian—and he laughed! You know the Lithuanian Jews—they rather despise books of devotion, but stuff themselves with the Talmud and the Codes. And who, I ask you, is going to argue with a *Litvack*?

What becomes of the Rebbe?

'I don't know, and I don't care', says he, shrugging his shoulders, and all the while (what it is to be a Lithuanian!) determined to find out!

The very same evening, soon after prayers, the Lithuanian steals into the Rebbe's room, lays himself down under the Rebbe's bed, and lies low. He intends to stay there all night, to find out where the Rebbe goes, and what he does at Sliches-time.

Day has not broken when he hears the call to prayer. The Rebbe has been awake some time. The Lithuanian has heard him sighing and groaning for a whole hour. Whoever has heard the groaning of the Nemirover Rebbe knows what sorrow for All-Israel, what distress of mind, found voice in every groan.

After that the Lithuanian hears the people rise and leave the house. Once more it is quiet and dark, only a very little moonlight comes in through the shutter. He confessed afterwards, did the Lithuanian, that when he found himself alone with the Rebbe, terror took hold of him. But a Lithuanian is dogged. He quivers and quakes like a fish, but he does not budge.

At last the Rebbe (long life to him!) rises in his turn. He goes to the wardrobe, and takes out a packet which proves to be the dress of a peasant: linen trousers, high boots, a pelisse, a wide felt hat, and a long and broad leather belt studded with brass nails. The Rebbe puts them on.

Out of the pockets of the pelisse dangles the end of a thick cord, a peasant's cord.

On his way out, the Rebbe steps aside into the kitchen, stoops, takes a hatchet from under the bed, puts it into his belt, and leaves the house. The Lithuanian trembles, but he persists.

A fearful Solemn Day hush broods over the dark streets, broken not infrequently by a cry of supplication from some little Minyan, or the moan of some sick person behind a window. The Rebbe keeps to the street side, and walks in the shadow of the houses. He glides from one to the other, the Lithuanian after him. And the Lithuanian hears the sound of his own heart-beats mingle with the heavy footfall of the Rebbe; but he follows on, and together they emerge from the town.

Behind the town stands a little wood. The Rebbe (long life to him!) enters it. He walks on thirty or forty paces, and then he stops beside a small tree. And the Lithuanian, with amazement, sees the Rebbe take his hatchet and strike the tree. He sees the Rebbe strike blow after blow, he hears the tree creak and snap. And the little tree falls, and the Rebbe splits it up into logs, and the logs into splinters. Then he makes a bundle, binds it round with the cord, throws it on his shoulder, replaces the hatchet in his belt, leaves the wood, and goes back into the town.

In one of the back streets he stops beside a poor, tumble-down little house, and taps at the window.

'Who is there?' cries a frightened voice within.

The Lithuanian knows it to be the voice of a Jewess, a sick Jewess.

'I', answers the Rebbe, in the peasant tongue.

'Who is I?' inquires the voice, further.

And the Rebbe answers again in the Little-Russian speech:

'Vassil.'

'Which Vassil? And what do you want, Vassil?'

'I have wood to sell', says the sham peasant, 'very cheap, for next to nothing.' And without further ado he goes in. The Lithuanian steals in behind him, and sees, in the grey light of dawn, a poor room with poor, broken furniture. In the bed lies a sick Jewess huddled up in rags, who says bitterly:

'Wood to sell—and where am I, a poor widow, to get money to buy it?'

'I will give you a six-groschen worth on credit.'

'And how am I ever to repay you?' groans the poor woman.

'Foolish creature!' the Rebbe upbraids her. 'See here: you are a poor sick Jewess, and I am willing to trust you with the little bundle of wood; I believe that in time you will repay me. And you, you have such a great, mighty God, and you do not trust Him! Not even to the amount of a miserable six groschen for a bundle of wood!'

'And who is to light the stove?' groans the widow. 'Do I look like getting up to do it, and my son away at work?'

'I will also light the stove for you', said the Rebbe. And the Rebbe, while he laid the wood in the stove, repeated, groaning, the first part of the Sliches. Then, when the stove was alight and the wood crackled cheerily, he repeated, more gaily, the second part of the Sliches. He repeated the third part when the fire had burnt itself out, and he shut the stove doors.

The Lithuanian, who saw all this, remained with the Rebbe as one of his followers.

And, later, when any one told how the Rebbe early every morning at Sliches-time raised himself and flew up into heaven, the Lithuanian, instead of laughing, added quietly:

'If not higher.'

J. L. PERETZ. (*Trans. Helena Frank.*)

---

1. Term for 'rabbi' among the Chassidim or Pietists of Eastern Europe.
2. Penitential Prayers before New Year and Atonement Day.
3. Temporary group of worshippers; also term for the quorum of ten males required for public worship.

DAY OF ATONEMENT

יו ם כ פ ו ר

TO Thee we give ourselves to-day,
　　Forgetful of the world outside;
We tarry in Thy house, O Lord,
From eventide to eventide.
From Thy all-searching, righteous eye
Our deepest heart can nothing hide;
It crieth up to Thee for peace
From eventide to eventide.
Who could endure, shouldst Thou, O God,
As we deserve, for ever chide?
We therefore seek Thy pardoning grace
From eventide to eventide.
O may we lay to heart how swift
The years of life do onward glide;
So learn to live that we may see
Thy light at our life's eventide.
G. GOTTHEIL.

FORGIVE thy neighbour the hurt that he hath done thee;

And then thy sins shall be pardoned when thou prayest.
Man cherisheth anger against man;
And doth he seek healing from the Lord?
Upon a man like himself he hath no mercy;
And doth he make supplication for his own sins?
ECCLESIASTICUS 28. 2–4.

THE MESSAGE OF YOM KIPPUR

IN large letters, so that even he that runs may read, does Yom Kippur spell forth the fundamentals of Judaism, of religion, of the higher life of man. Sin is not an evil power whose chains the children of flesh must helplessly drag towards a weary tomb. We can always shake off its yoke; and what is more, we need never assume its yoke. An ancient fable tells us of distant oceans with mountainous rocks of magnet of such terrific power that wreck and ruin befell any ship venturing near them. Instantly the iron nails would fly out of the ship, bolts and fastenings would be torn away by that magnetic force; the vessel would become nothing more than so many planks of wood, and all on board fall a prey to the hungry waters. Sins there are that, likewise, unhinge all our stays of character, rob us of the restraints of past habits and education, and leave us helpless playthings on the billows of temptation and passion. Yet a man is the pilot of his life's barque, and can at all times steer it so as never to come near those mountains of destruction and death.

And, secondly, there is an atonement for man's sins. We may repair the ravages of sin, rebuild the shifting foundations of character, and join again the sundered strands of our spiritual fabric. We spurn the old pagan fatalism which declares that there is no forgiveness for sin. Nature provides some escape from physical disease; shall the soul, injured by temptation's fire, scarred by sin, not be able to recover its pristine strength and beauty? No matter how harsh nature and man may seem, the God of Eternal Right holds a deep pity that can atone and save, bury not only sin, but its grave and graveyard with it!

As clear as a bell resounds the third and greatest teaching of Yom Kippur: man himself must prepare himself for atonement, and no priest or mediator can prepare or work atonement for him. Virtue is victory by the individual himself over temptation that assails him. The battle cannot be fought nor the victory won by another. The human soul, wandering on the devious labyrinthine paths of sin, must itself essay to forsake the Way of Sorrow and proceed on the Way of Salvation. This is the most splendid, the most momentous fact in human life: that though man cannot always even half control his destiny, God has given the reins of man's conduct altogether into his hands.

No wonder that the Synagogue has ever looked upon this day of prayer, fasting, and humiliation as a *festival*. A generation or two ago our forefathers stood robed in white in the Synagogue, during the entire Atonement Day. Originally these white garments were not worn as reminders of the grave; they were an outward sign of the festal character of this Day, appointed for life's spiritual renewal. 'When men are summoned before an earthly ruler', says the Jerusalem Talmud, 'to defend themselves against some charge, they appear downcast and dressed in black like mourners. Israel appears before God on the Atonement Day attired in white as if going to a feast, because he is confident that as soon as he returns penitently to his Maker, He will not condemn, but will abundantly pardon.'

J. H. HERTZ, 1900.

'FORGIVEN'

אָמְנָם כֵּן יֵצֶר סוֹבֵל חַטָּאתִי

1

RAISE to Thee this my plea, take my pray'r,
Sin unmake for Thy sake and declare,
'Forgiven!'
Tears, regret, witness set in sin's place;
Uplift trust from the dust to Thy face—
'Forgiven!'
Voice that sighs, tear-filled eyes, do not spurn;
Weigh and pause, plead my cause, and return
'Forgiven!'
Yea, off-rolled—as foretold—clouds impure,
Zion's folk, free of yoke, O assure
'Forgiven!'
YOMTOB OF YORK, 1190. (*Trans. I. Zangwill.*)

---

1. From *Service of the Synagogue* (Geo. Routledge & Sons).

CONFESSION

תְּרָ מַ_ל_ֶכ·ות

S HAME-STRICKEN, bending low,
  My God, I come before Thee, for I know
That even as Thou on high
Exalted art in power and majesty,
So weak and frail am I:
That perfect as Thou art,
So I deficient am in every part.
Thou art all-wise, all-good, all-great, divine,
Yea, Thou art God: eternity is Thine;
While I, a thing of clay,
The creature of a day,
Pass shadow-like, a breath, that comes and flees away.
My God, I know my sins are numberless,
More than I can recall to memory
Or tell their tale: yet some will I confess,
Even a few, though as a drop it be
In all the sea.
I will declare my trespasses and sin,
And peradventure silence then may fall
Upon their waves and billows' raging din,

And Thou wilt hear from heaven, when I call,
And pardon all.
My God, if mine iniquity
Too great for all endurance be,
Yet for Thy name's sake pardon me.
For if in Thee I may not dare
To hope, who else will hear my prayer?
Therefore, although Thou slay me, yet
In Thee my faith and trust is set:
And though Thou seekest out my sin,
From Thee to Thee I fly to win
A place of refuge, and within
Thy shadow from Thy anger hide,
Until Thy wrath be turned aside.
Unto Thy mercy I will cling
Until Thou hearken, pitying:
Nor will I quit my hold of Thee
Until Thy blessing light on me.
Remember, O my God, I pray,
How Thou hast formed me out of clay,
What troubles set upon my way.
Do Thou not, then, my deeds requite
According to my sins aright,
But with Thy mercy infinite.
For well I know, through good and ill,
That Thou in love hast chastened still,
Afflicting me in faithfulness,
That Thou my latter end may'st bless.
SOLOMON IBN GABIROL, 1050. (*Trans. Alice Lucas.*)

YOM KIPPUR MEDITATIONS

I

MY soul, be not senseless, like a beast, deeply sunk;—be not drowsy, with passion drunk.—Hewn from reason's mind thou art;—from wisdom's well thy waters start,—from the Lord's heavenly realm!

My soul, let not the body's wanton pleasures capture thee,—its showy treasures not enrapture thee;—they melt away—like the dew before the day,—they avail naught when they begin,—and their end is shame and sin.

My soul, look carefully back—on thy pilgrim's track;—all cometh from the dust,—and thither return it must.—Whatever has been moulded and built,—when its time is fulfilled,—must go back to the ground—where its material was found.—Death is life's brother.—They keep fast to one another,—each taking hold of one end of their plunder, —and none can tear them asunder.—Soon thou wilt come—to thine eternal home,—where thou must show thy work and receive thy wages —on rightful scales and gauges,—or good or bad, according to the worth—of thy deeds on earth.

Therefore get thee up, and to thy Master pray—by night and day;— bow down before Him, be meek,—and let thy tears bedew thy cheek. —Seek the Lord, thy Light,—with all thy might;—walk in meekness, pursue the right;—so that with His mercy-screen the Master—hide thee in the day of disaster.—Then thou shalt shine like the heavens bright, —and like the sun when going forth in might;—and o'er thy head— shall be spread—the rays—of the sun of grace—that brings—healing and joy in his wings.

BACHYA IBN PAKUDAH, 1040. (*Trans. M. Jastrow.*)

II

FORGET thine anguish,
Vexed heart, again.
Why shouldst thou languish,
With earthly pain?
The husk shall slumber,
Bedded in clay,
Silent and sombre,
Oblivion's prey.
But, Spirit immortal,
Thou at Death's portal
Tremblest with fear.
If he caress thee,
Curse thee, or bless thee,
Thou must draw near,
From him the worth of thy works to hear.
Why, full of terror,
Compassed with error,
Trouble thy heart
For thy mortal part?
The soul flies home—
The corpse is dumb.
Of all thou didst have
Follows naught to the grave.
Thou fliest thy nest,
Swift as a bird to thy place of rest.
Life is a vine-branch;
A vintager, Death.
He threatens and lowers
More near with each breath.

Then hasten, arise!
Seek God, O my soul!
For time quickly flies,
Still far is the goal.
Vain heart praying dumbly,
Learn to prize humbly
The meanest of fare.
Forget all thy sorrow,
Behold, death is there!
Dove-like lamenting,
Be full of repenting;
Lift vision supernal
To raptures eternal;
On every occasion
Seek lasting salvation.
Pour thy heart out in weeping
While others are sleeping.
Pray to Him when all's still,
Performing His will.
And so shall the Angel of Peace be thy warden,
And guide thee at last to the heavenly garden.
SOLOMON IBN GABIROL, 1050. (*Trans. Emma Lazarus*).

THE INFINITE MERCIES
OF GOD

THE Lord, the Lord is a merciful and gracious God, slow to anger and abounding in lovingkindness and truth; keeping lovingkindness for thousands, forgiving iniquity and transgression and sin.

EXODUS 34. 6, 7.

MAY it be Thy will, O God, that we return to Thee in perfect penitence, so that we may not be ashamed to meet our fathers in the life to come.

Unite our hearts, O God, to fear Thy name; keep us far from what Thou hatest; bring us near to what Thou lovest; and deal mercifully with us for Thy name's sake.

May it be Thy will, O God, that love and peace and brotherliness dwell among us! May our hopes of Heaven be fulfilled! Grant that the good inclination may uphold us. Fill us with the desire to fear Thy name, and do Thou give us our soul's peace. Amen.

TALMUD.

BROTHERHOOD

A T the beginning of the Atonement service the most venerable men in the congregation solemnly repeat from the Almemor[1]: 'With the permission of the Court on High, and with the permission of the Congregation below, we declare it permitted to pray with hardened transgressors'. Why this custom? In some communities of the Middle Ages there were persons who, by their conduct, had placed themselves outside the pale of Judaism; cowardly apostates, for example, who sold their souls; informers, who spread broadcast false accusations against their brethren; insubordinates, outcasts, criminals. Throughout the year these never sought spiritual fellowship with their brethren. On Yom Kippur, however, they would steal into some corner of the synagogue and join the worshippers in prayer. The Rabbis thereupon instituted this solemn declaration, in order to proclaim in most unmistakable terms that, no matter what is a man's mode of life— slanderer, apostate, outcast—he is still a brother. '*We* have transgressed, *we* have dealt treacherously, *we* have robbed,' do we pray. We associate ourselves with the most forlorn souls that sin in darkness, because we recognize that society—we ourselves—are largely responsible for their actions. Many a time has our evil example misled others, and become a stumbling-block in the way of the blind. And all our Yom Kippur vows to rise to a higher life are useless, unless we endeavour to raise others who have fallen. A traveller was crossing mountain heights of untrodden snow alone. He struggled bravely against the sense of sleep which weighed down his eyelids, but it was fast stealing over him, and he knew that if he fell asleep death would inevitably follow. At this crisis his foot struck against a heap lying across his path. Stooping down, he found it to be a human body half buried in the snow. The next moment he held him in his arms, and was rubbing and chafing the frozen man's limbs. The effort to restore another unto life brought back to himself warmth and energy, and was the means of saving both. The same law obtains in the realm of the soul. In order that our spiritual vitality may quicken into new life, we must help others in highest matters of faith and hope.

'Heaven's gate is shut
To him who comes alone;
Save thou a soul,
And it shall save thine own.'
J. H. HERTZ, 1898.

I WILL seek that which is lost, and will bring again that which is driven away, and will bind up that which is broken, and will strengthen that which is sick.
EZEKIEL 34. 16.

---

1. Reading Desk, usually in the centre of the Synagogue.

ATONEMENT PROMISE
AND ADMONITION

I

S EEK ye the Lord while He may be found,
    Call ye upon Him while He is near;
Let the wicked forsake his way,
And the man of iniquity his thoughts;
And let him return unto the Lord,
And He will have compassion upon him,
And to our God, for He will abundantly pardon.
For My thoughts are not your thoughts,
Neither are your ways My ways, saith the Lord.
For as the heavens are higher than the earth,
So are My ways higher than your ways,
And My thoughts than your thoughts.
For as the rain cometh down and the snow from heaven,
And returneth not thither,
Except it water the earth,
And make it bring forth and bud,
And give seed to the sower and bread to the eater;
So shall My word be that goeth forth out of My mouth:
It shall not return unto Me void,
Except it accomplish that which I please,

And make the thing whereto I sent it prosper.
ISAIAH 55. 6–11.

II

THEN shall thy light break forth as the morning,
    And thy healing shall spring forth speedily;
    And thy righteousness shall go before thee,
    The glory of the Lord shall be thy rearward.
    Then shalt thou call, and the Lord shall answer;
    Thou shalt cry, and He will say: 'Here I am.'
    If thou take away from the midst of thee the yoke,
    The putting forth of the finger, and speaking wickedness;
    And if thou draw out thy soul to the hungry,
    And satisfy the afflicted soul;
    Then shall thy light rise in darkness,
    And thy gloom be as the noonday;
    And the Lord will guide thee continually,
    And satisfy thy soul in drought,
    And make strong thy bones;
    And thou shalt be like a watered garden,
    And like a spring of water, whose waters fail not.
    And they that shall be of thee shall build the old waste places,
    Thou shalt raise up the foundations of many generations;
    And thou shalt be called The repairer of the breach, The restorer of
paths to dwell in.
    ISAIAH 58. 8–12.

LORD, THINE HUMBLE
SERVANTS HEAR

L ORD, thine humble servants hear,
     Suppliant now before Thee;
Our Father, from Thy children's plea
Turn not, we implore Thee!
Lord, blot out our evil pride,
All our sins before Thee;
Our Father, for Thy Mercy's sake,
Pardon, we implore Thee.
Lord, no sacrifice we bring,
Prayers and tears implore Thee;
Our Father, take the gift we lay,
Contrite hearts before Thee.
Lord, Thy sheep have wandered far,
Gather them before Thee;
Our Father, let Thy shepherd's love
Guide us, we implore Thee.
Lord, forgive and comfort all
That in truth implore Thee;
Our Father, let our evening prayer
Thus find grace before Thee.
R. YEHUDAH. (*Trans. S. Solis-Cohen.*)

GOD THAT DOEST WONDROUSLY

G OD, that doest wondrously,
    God, that doest wondrously,
Pardon at Thy people's cry,
As the closing hour draws nigh!
Few are Israel's sons, and weak;
Thee, in penitence, they seek.
O regard their anguished cry,
As the closing hour draws nigh!
Souls in grief before Thee poured,
Agonize for deed and word;
'We have sinned. Forgive!' they cry,
As the closing hour draws nigh!
Heal them! Let their trust in Thee
Turn aside Wrath's dread decree;
Doom them not, but heed their cry,
As the closing hour draws nigh!
For our Fathers' righteousness
Save us now in our distress;
Make us glad with freedom's cry,
As the closing hour draws nigh!
R. MOSHEH. (*Trans. S. Solis-Cohen.*)

TABERNACLES

זְמַן שִׂמְחָתֵנוּ

T HE divine religion does not urge us to lead an ascetic life, but guides us in the middle path, equidistant from the extremes of too much and too little; it allows free play to every God-given faculty of both body and soul, within the limits drawn by the Divine Hand itself. For certain it is that what we devote to one faculty in excessive measure we withdraw from another faculty, and thus lose the harmony which should pervade our whole life. In general, let me impress this principle upon thy mind: the essence of our whole law is contained in these three things—reverence, love, joy. They are the way to bring us near to God. Thy contrition on the day of fasting is in no wise more pleasing to Him than thy joy on the sabbath or the festival, if so be that thy delight comes from a devout and full heart. Just as prayer requires reflection and devotion, so does joy in God's commandments and the study of His revelation. Thou must rejoice in the love of Him who gave the Law, being persuaded that the giving thereof was an act of His love towards thee.

YEHUDAH HALEVI, 1141.

PALMS AND MYRTLES

THY praise, O Lord, will I proclaim
    In hymns unto Thy glorious name.
O Thou Redeemer, Lord and King,
Redemption to Thy faithful bring!
Before Thine altar they rejoice
With branch of palm and myrtle-stem;
To Thee they raise the prayerful voice—
Have mercy, save and prosper them.
They overflow with prayer and praise
To Him who knows the future days.
Have mercy Thou, and hear the prayer
Of those who palms and myrtles bear.
Thee day and night they sanctify
And in perpetual song adore;
Like to the heavenly host, they cry,
'Blessed art Thou for evermore'.
ELEAZAR KALIR, 8th cent. (*Trans. Alice Lucas.*)

THE HARVEST FESTIVAL

I N keeping in view the agricultural aspect of the Three Festivals, the modern Jew performs no unimportant duty. He realizes the fact that Israel was once a people who lived by tilling the soil, and that the commercial character which so largely distinguishes his people in these times is not, as is commonly thought, inborn, but is the result of the unkindly conditions in which they have been compelled to live. It is good for us and the world at large to remember that the history of our race has its idyllic side.

MORRIS JOSEPH, 1903.

THE vineyards of Israel have ceased to exist, but the eternal Law enjoins the children of Israel still to celebrate the vintage. A race that persist in celebrating their vintage, although they have no fruits to gather, will regain their vineyards.

BENJAMIN DISRAELI, 1846.

JOYOUS SERVICE

T HE easily depressed, the despondent and morose man has often become what he is from mere selfishness. It is so delightful to pity ourselves, to yield to the 'luxury of woe', and sing a plaintive song of self-commiseration in a minor key. But the next step is to give your soul to the devil. Judaism is not more emphatic against the latter than the former, and I am sure that there are few wickeder thoughts than this: that God made me with a despondent, melancholy heart. Shammai said: 'Always be cheerful'. R. Ishmael said: 'Ever be joyful'. This Rabbi Ishmael died a martyr's death in the second century of this era. Do you think that when he suffered he repined and said: 'If I had known how my life was to end I would have wept my days away instead of joyously doing my duty'? Serve the Lord with gladness, and the gladness will leave its after-glow of resignation, contentment, and peace.

I. ABRAHAMS, 1893.

THE Spirit of God abideth not where there is either needless grieving or inactivity; but only where there is *joyful* performance of duty.

TALMUD.

REJOICING OF THE LAW

THIS Feast of the Law all your gladness display,
    To-day all your homages render.
What profit can lead one so pleasant a way,
What jewels can vie with its splendour?
Then exult in the Law on its festival day,
The Law is our Light and Defender.
My God I will praise in a jubilant lay,
My hope in Him never surrender,
His glory proclaim where His chosen sons pray,
My Rock all my trust shall engender.
Then exult in the Law on its festival day,
The Law is our Light and Defender.
My heart of Thy goodness shall carol alway,
Thy praises I ever will render;
While breath is, my lips all Thy wonders shall say,
Thy truth and Thy kindness so tender.
Then exult in the Law on its festival day,
The Law is our Light and Defender.
FESTIVAL PRAYER BOOK. (*Trans. I. Zangwill.*)

SIMCHAS TORAH

LECHAYIM,[1] my brethren, Lechayim, I say,
   Health, peace, and good fortune I wish you to-day.
To-day we have ended the Torah once more;
To-day we begin it anew, as of yore.
Be thankful and glad and the Lord extol,
Who gave us the Law on its parchment scroll.
The Torah has been our consolation,
Our help in exile and sore privation.
Lost have we all we were wont to prize:
Our holy temple a ruin lies;
Laid waste is the land where our songs we sung;
Forgotten our language, our mother-tongue;
Of kingdom and priesthood are we bereft;
Our Faith is our only treasure left.
God in our hearts, the Law in our hands,
We have wandered sadly through many lands.
We have suffered much; yet, behold, we live
Through the comfort the Law alone can give.
Two thousand years, a little thing when spoken;
Two thousand years tormented, crushed, and broken
Seven and seventy dark generations
Filled up with anguish and lamentations!

Their tale of sorrow did I unfold,
No *Simchas Torah* to-day we'd hold.
And why should I tell it you all again?
In our bones 'tis branded with fire and pain.
We have sacrificed all. We have given our wealth,
Our homes, our honours, our land, our health,
Our lives—like Hannah her children seven—
For the sake of the Torah that came from heaven.
And now, what next? Will they let us be?
Have the nations then come at last to see
That we Jews are men like the rest, and no more
Need we wander homeless as heretofore,
Abused and slandered wherever we go?
Ah! I cannot tell you. But this I know,
That the same God still lives in heaven above,
And on earth the same Law, the same Faith, that we love.
Then fear not, and weep not, but hope in the Lord,
And the sacred Torah, his Holy Word.
Lechayim, my brethren, Lechayim, I say!
Health, peace, and good fortune I wish you to-day.
To-day we have ended the Torah once more;
To-day we begin it again, as of yore.
Be thankful and glad and the Lord extol,
Who gave us the Law on its parchment scroll.
J. L. GORDON. (*Trans. Alice Lucas and Helena Frank.*)

—————————————————————

1. 'Your health!'

THE MACCABEAN
WARRIORS

T hey were ready either to live or die nobly.
1 MACCABEES 4. 35.

AND King Antiochus wrote to his whole kingdom, that all should be one people, and that each should forsake his own laws. And he sent letters unto Jerusalem and the cities of Judah that they should profane the sabbaths and feasts, pollute the sanctuary, and build altars and temples and shrines for idols; and whosoever shall not do according to the word of the king, he shall die. And he appointed overseers over all the people, and he commanded the cities of Judah to sacrifice, city by city. And they did evil things in the land; and they made Israel to hide themselves in every place of refuge which they had. And they rent in pieces the Books of the Law which they found, and set them on fire. And wheresoever was found with any a Book of the Covenant, and if any consented to the Law, the king's sentence delivered him to death.

And in those days rose up Mattathias, a priest from Jerusalem; and he dwelt at Modin. And he had five sons, John, Simon, Judas (who was called Maccabaeus), Eleazar, Jonathan. And he saw the blasphemies that were committed in Judah and in Jerusalem, and Mattathias and his sons rent their clothes, and put on sackcloth, and mourned exceedingly.

And the king's officers, that were enforcing the apostasy, came into the city Modin. And many of Israel came unto them, and Mattathias and his sons were gathered together. And the king's officers spake to Mattathias, saying, 'Thou art a ruler and an honourable and great man in this city, and strengthened with sons and brethren; now therefore come thou first and do the commandment of the king, as all nations have done, and the men of Judah, and they that remain in Jerusalem; so shalt thou and thy house be in the number of the king's Friends, and thou and thy children shall be honoured with silver and gold, and many rewards.' And Mattathias answered and said with a loud voice, *'Though all the nations that are under the king's dominion obey him, and fall away every one from the religion of their fathers, yet will I and my sons and my brethren walk in the covenant of our fathers.'* And Mattathias cried out in the city with a loud voice, saying, 'Whosoever is zealous for the Law, and maintaineth the Covenant, let him follow me.'

Then were gathered together unto them every one that offered himself willingly for the Law. And all they that fled from the evils were added to them, and became a stay unto them. And they mustered a host, and pulled down the altars; and they pursued after the sons of pride, neither suffered they the sinner to triumph.

Selection from 1 MACCABEES 1. 41–2. 48.

THE FEAST OF LIGHTS

K INDLE the taper like the steadfast star,
  Ablaze on evening's forehead o'er the earth,
And add each night a lustre till afar
An eightfold splendour shine above thy hearth.
Clash, Israel, the cymbals, touch the lyre,
Blow the brass trumpet and the harsh-tongued horn;
Chant psalms of victory till the heart takes fire,
The Maccabean spirit leap new-born.
EMMA LAZARUS.

THE MENORAH

D EEP in his soul he began to feel the need of being a Jew. His circumstances were not unsatisfactory; he enjoyed an ample income and a profession that permitted him to do whatever his heart desired. For he was an artist. His Jewish origin and the faith of his fathers had long since ceased to trouble him, when suddenly the old hatred came to the surface again in a new mob-cry. With many others he believed that this flood would shortly subside. But there was no change for the better; and every blow, even though not aimed directly at him, struck him with fresh pain, till little by little his soul became one bleeding wound. These sorrows, buried deep in his heart and silenced there, evoked thoughts of their origin and of his Judaism; and now he did something he could not perhaps have done in the old days —he began to love his Judaism with an intense fervour. Although in his own eyes he could not, at first, clearly justify this new yearning, it became so powerful at length that it crystallized from vague emotions into a definite idea which he must needs express. It was the conviction that there was only one solution for this moral misery—the return to Judaism.

The Jew of to-day had lost the poise which was his fathers' very being. This generation, having grown up under the influence of alien cultures, was no longer capable of that return which he had perceived to be their redemption. But the new generation would be capable of it, if it were only given the right direction early enough. He resolved, therefore, that his own children, at least, should be shown the proper path. They should be trained as Jews in their own home.

Hitherto he had permitted to pass by unobserved the holiday which the wonderful apparition of the Maccabees had illumined for thousands of years with the glow of miniature lights. Now, however, he made this holiday an opportunity to prepare something beautiful which should be for ever commemorated in the minds of his children. In their young souls should be implanted early a steadfast devotion to their ancient people. He bought a Menorah, and when he held this nine-branched candlestick in his hands for the first time, a strange mood came over him. In his father's house also the lights had once burned in his youth, now far away, and the recollection gave him a sad and tender feeling for home. The tradition was neither cold nor dead—thus it had passed through the ages, one light kindling another. Moreover, the ancient form of the Menorah had excited his interest. Clearly the design was suggested by the tree—in the centre the sturdy trunk, on right and left four branches, one below the other, in one place, and all of equal height. A later symbolism brought with it the short ninth branch, which projects in front and functions as a servant. What mystery had the generations which followed one another read into this form of art, at once so simple and natural! And our artist wondered to himself if it were not possible to animate again the withered form of the Menorah —to water its roots, as one would a tree. The mere sound of the name, which he now pronounced every evening to his children, gave him great pleasure. There was a lovable ring to the word when it came from the lips of little children.

On the first night the candle was lit and the origin of the holiday explained. The wonderful incident of the lights that strangely remained burning so long, the story of the return from the Babylonian exile, the second Temple, the Maccabees—our friend told his children all he knew. It was not very much, to be sure; but it served. When the second candle was lit, they repeated what he had told them; and though it had all been learnt from him, it seemed to him quite new and beautiful. In the days that followed, he waited keenly for the evenings which became ever brighter. Candle after candle stood in the Menorah, and the father mused on the little candles with his children till at length his reflections became too deep to be uttered before them.

Then came the eighth day, when the whole row burns, even the faithful ninth, the servant, which on other nights is used only for the lighting of the others. A great splendour streamed from the Menorah. The children's eyes glistened. But for our friend all this was the symbol of the enkindling of a nation. When there is but one light, all is still dark, and the solitary light looks melancholy. Soon it finds one companion, then another, and another. The darkness must retreat. The light comes first to the young and the poor—then others join who love Justice, Truth, Liberty, Progress, Humanity, and Beauty. When all the candles burn, then we must all stand and rejoice over the achievement. And no office can be more blessed than that of a Servant of the Light.

THEODOR HERZL. (*Trans. B. L. Pouzzner.*)

THE STORY OF THE
MACCABEES

I T is good for Jewish lads to include warriors of their own race in their gallery of heroes, to be able to say, 'My people has produced its brave men equally with the Greeks and the Romans'.

But still better it is for them to feel that these brave men drew their courage from the purest of all sources, from a passionate love for their religion, from a veneration for the good and the true and the morally beautiful. The Maccabees boldly faced overwhelming odds, not for their own selfish ends, but in a spirit of self-sacrificing fidelity to the holiest of all causes. They threw themselves upon the enemy in the temper that takes the martyr to the stake; they did it not for gain or glory, but solely for conscience' sake. They felt that God was calling to them, and they could not hold back. Theirs was a unique effort. Others had, it is true, displayed an equally noble courage on the battle-field. But what they had fought for was their fatherland and their mother tongue, their hearths and homes. To fight for Religion was a new thing.

The little Maccabean band was like a rock in the midst of a surging sea. Standing almost alone in their day, the heroes beat back the forces that threatened to involve all mankind in a common demoralization. They kept a corner of the world sweet in an impure age. They held aloft the torch of true religion at a time when thick darkness was covering the nations.

MORRIS JOSEPH, 1903.

CHANUCAH HYMN

ROCK of Ages, let our song
    Praise Thy saving power;
Thou, amidst the raging foes,
Wast our shelt'ring tower.
Furious they assailed us,
But Thine arm availed us;
And Thy word
Broke their sword
When our own strength failed us.
Kindling new the holy lamps,
Priests approved in suffering
Purified the nation's shrine,
Brought to God their offering.
And His courts surrounding
Hear, in joy abounding,
Happy throngs
Singing songs
With a mighty sounding.
Children of the Martyr-race,
Whether free or fettered,
Wake the echoes of the songs
Where ye may be scattered.

Yours the message cheering,
That the time is nearing
Which shall see
All men free,
Tyrants disappearing.
G. GOTTHEIL.

PURIM

THERE was a certain Jew in Shushan ... whose name was Mordecai.... And he brought up Hadassah, that is, Esther, his uncle's daughter ... and when her father and mother were dead, Mordecai took her for his own daughter.... And Esther was taken unto King Ahasuerus into his house royal ... and the king loved Esther ... and she obtained grace and favour in his sight....

After these things did King Ahasuerus promote Haman, and set his seat above all the princes that were with him. And Haman said, 'There is a certain people scattered abroad and dispersed among the peoples in all the provinces of thy kingdom; and their laws are diverse from those of every people, neither keep they the king's laws: therefore it is not for the king's profit to suffer them. If it please the king let it be written that they be destroyed ... both young and old, little children and women, in one day.' And the king said unto Haman, 'The people is given to thee to do with them as it seemeth good to thee'.

Now, when Mordecai knew all that was done he rent his clothes ... and charged Esther that she should go in unto the king to make supplication unto him for her people—'Think not with thyself that thou shalt escape in the king's house, more than all the Jews. For if thou altogether holdest thy peace at this time, then shall relief and deliverance arise to the Jews from another place: and who knoweth whether thou art not come to the kingdom for such a time as this?' ... Esther bade them return answer unto Mordecai, 'So will I go in unto the king ... and if I perish, I perish....'

Then Esther the queen ... said, 'If I have found favour in thy sight, O king ... let my life be given me at my petition, and my people at my request; for we are sold, I and my people, to be destroyed, to be slain and to perish....' Then spake the king Ahasuerus, 'Who is he, and where is he, that durst presume in his heart to do so?' And Esther said, 'An adversary and an enemy, even this wicked Haman'.

Then said one of the chamberlains, 'Behold also, the gallows which Haman hath made for Mordecai, who spake good for the king (and saved the king's life) standeth in the house of Haman'. And the king said, 'Hang him thereon'. So they hanged Haman.... And the king said, 'Write ye also to the Jews as it liketh you, in the king's name....' The Jews had light and gladness and joy and honour. And whithersoever the king's commandment and his decree came, the Jews had gladness and joy....

... Therefore do the Jews ... make the fourteenth day of the month Adar a day of gladness and feasting ... and of sending gifts to the poor.

BOOK OF ESTHER.

SERVANT OF GOD

S PIRIT and flesh are Thine,
    O Heavenly Shepherd mine;
My hopes, my thoughts, my fears, Thou seest all,
Thou measurest my path, my steps dost know.
When Thou upholdest, who can make me fall?
When Thou restrainest, who can bid me go?
O would that I might be
A servant unto Thee,
Thou God, by all adored!
Then, though by friends out-cast,
Thy hand would hold me fast,
And draw me near to Thee, my King and Lord!
Fain would my heart come nigh
To Thee, O God, on high,
But evil thoughts have led me far astray
From the pure path of righteous government.
Guide Thou me back into Thy holy way,
And count me not as one impenitent.
O would that I might be
A servant unto Thee,
Thou God, by all adored!
Then, though by friends out-cast,

Thy hand would hold me fast,
And draw me near to Thee, my King and Lord!
Contrite and full of dread,
I mourn each moment fled,
'Midst idle follies roaming desolate:
I sink beneath transgressions manifold,
That from Thy presence keep me separate,
Nor can sin-darkened eyes Thy light behold.
O would that I might be
A servant unto Thee,
Thou God, by all adored!
Then, though by friends out-cast,
Thy hand would hold me fast,
And draw me near to Thee, my King and Lord!
So lead me that I may
Thy sovereign will obey.
Make pure my heart to seek Thy truth divine;
When burns my wound, be Thou with healing near!
Answer me, Lord! for sore distress is mine,
And say unto Thy servant, I am here.
O would that I might be
A servant unto Thee,
Thou God, by all adored!
Then, though by friends out-cast,
Thy hand would hold me fast,
And draw me near to Thee, my King and Lord!
YEHUDAH HALEVI, 1140. (*Trans. Alice Lucas.*)

HYMN OF GLORY

S WEET hymns and songs will I indite
  To sing of Thee by day and night—
Of Thee, who art my soul's delight.
How doth my soul within me yearn
Beneath Thy shadow to return,
Thy secret mysteries to learn!
And even while yet Thy glory fires
My words, and hymns of praise inspires,
Thy love it is my heart desires.
Thy glory shall my discourse be;
In images I picture Thee,
Although Thyself I cannot see.
O Thou whose word is truth alway,
Thy people seek Thy face this day;
O be Thou near them when they pray.
O may my words of blessing rise
To Thee, who, throned above the skies,
Art just and mighty, great and wise.
My meditation day and night,
May it be pleasant in Thy sight,
For Thou art all my soul's delight.
JUDAH THE PIOUS, 12th cent. (*Trans. Alice Lucas.*)

THE VOICE OF WISDOM

THUS saith the Lord, Let not the wise man glory in his wisdom, neither the mighty man glory in his might, let not the rich man glory in his riches; but let him that glorieth glory in this, that he understandeth and knoweth Me, that I am the Lord who exercise loving kindness, judgement, and righteousness in the earth: for in these things I delight, saith the Lord.
    JEREMIAH 9. 23–4.

HE that planted the ear, shall He not hear? He that formed the eye, shall He not see? He that instructeth the nations, shall not He correct, Even He that teacheth man knowledge?
    PSALM 94. 9–10.

GOD, WHOM SHALL
I COMPARE TO THEE!

G OD, whom shall I compare to Thee,
    When Thou to none canst likened be?
Under what image shall I dare
To picture Thee, when everywhere
All Nature's forms Thine impress bear?
Hearts, seeking Thee, from search refrain,
And weary tongues their praise restrain.
Thyself unbound by time and place,
Thou dost pervade, support, embrace
The world and all created space.
Deep, deep beyond all fathoming,
Far, far beyond all measuring,
We can but seek Thy deeds alone;
When bow Thy saints before Thy throne
Then is Thy faithfulness made known.
Thy righteousness we can discern,
Thy holy law proclaim and learn.
Is not Thy presence near alway
To them who penitently pray,
But far from those who sinning stray?
Pure souls behold Thee, and no need
Have they of light: they hear and heed

Thee with the mind's keen ear, although
The ear of flesh be dull and slow.
Their voices answer to and fro.
Thy holiness for ever they proclaim:
The Lord of Hosts! thrice holy is His name.
YEHUDAH HALEVI. (*Trans. Alice Lucas.*)

GREAT IS TRUTH

G REAT is Truth, and stronger than all things. All the earth calleth upon Truth, and the heaven blesseth her; all works shake and tremble, but with her is no unrighteous thing.... Truth abideth, and is strong for ever; she liveth and conquereth for evermore.... She is the strength, and the kingdom, and the power, and the majesty, of all ages. Blessed be the God of Truth.

1 ESDRAS 4. 35, 36, 38, 40.

TRUTH is the seal of God.
TALMUD.

THE RIGHT LIFE

I T hath been told thee, O man, what is good, and what the Lord doth require of thee: only to do justly, and to love mercy, and to walk humbly with thy God.

MICAH 6. 8.

WOE unto them that call evil good, and good evil; that put darkness for light, and light for darkness; that put bitter for sweet, and sweet for bitter!

Woe unto them that are wise in their own eyes, and prudent in their own sight!

ISAIAH 5. 20-2.

THE proper study of a wise man is not how to die, but how to live.

A man who desires to help others by counsel or deed will refrain from dwelling on men's faults, and will speak but sparingly of human weaknesses. But he will speak at large of man's virtue and power, and the means of perfecting the same, that thus men may endeavour joyously to live, so far as in them lies, after the commandment of reason.

BENEDICT SPINOZA, 1674.

THE GOODNESS OF
GOD'S WORK

M EN frequently think that the evils in the world are more numerous than the good things; many sayings and songs of the nations dwell on this idea. They say that the good is found only exceptionally, whilst evil things are numerous and lasting. The origin of this error is to be found in the circumstance that men judge of the *whole universe* by examining one single person only. If anything happens to him contrary to his expectation, forthwith they conclude that the whole universe is evil. All mankind at present in existence forms only an infinitesimal portion of the permanent universe. It is of great advantage that man should know his station. Numerous evils to which persons are exposed are due to the defects existing in the persons themselves. We seek relief from our own faults; we suffer from evils which we inflict on ourselves, and we ascribe them to God who is far from connected with them. As Solomon explained it: The foolishness of man perverteth his way, and his heart fretteth against the Lord.

MOSES MAIMONIDES, 1190.

THE TWO NATURES
IN MAN

IT is because man is half angel, half brute, that his inner life witnesses such bitter war between such unlike natures. The brute in him clamours for sensual joy and things in which there is only vanity; but the angel resists and strives to make him know that meat, drink, sleep are but means whereby the body may be made efficient for the study of the truths, and the doing of the will, of God. Not until the very hour of death can it be certain or known to what measure the victory has been won. He who is but a novice in the fear of God will do well to say audibly each day, as he rises: 'This day I will be a faithful servant of the Almighty. I will be on my guard against wrath, falsehood, hatred, and quarrelsomeness, and will forgive those who wound me.' For whoso forgives is forgiven in his turn; hard-heartedness and a temper that will not make up quarrels are a heavy burden of sin, and unworthy of an Israelite.

MOSES OF COUCY, 13th cent.

FREEDOM OF THE WILL

F REE will is granted to every man. If he desire to incline towards the good way and be righteous, he has the power to do so; and if he desire to incline towards the unrighteous way and be a wicked man, he has also the power to do so. Give no room in your minds to that which is asserted by heathen fools, and also by many of the ignorant among the Israelites themselves, namely: that the Holy One, blessed be He, decrees that a man from his birth should be either a righteous man or a wicked man.

Since the power of doing good or evil is in our own hands, and since all the wicked deeds which we have committed have been committed with our full consciousness, it befits us to turn in penitence and to forsake our evil deeds; the power of doing so being still in our hands. Now this matter is a very important principle; nay, it is the pillar of the Law and of the commandments.

MOSES MAIMONIDES, 1180.

THE WICKED SAITH IN
HIS HEART

F OR they said within themselves, reasoning not aright,
    'Short and sorrowful is our life;
And there is no healing when a man cometh to his end,
And none was ever known that returned out of Hades.
Because by mere chance were we born,
And hereafter we shall be as though we had never been:
And our name shall be forgotten in time,
And no man shall remember our works;
And our life shall pass away as the traces of a cloud,
And shall be scattered as is a mist.
For our allotted time is the passing of a shadow,
And there is no putting back of our end.
Come therefore and let us enjoy the good things that now are;
And let us use the creation with all our soul as youth's possession.
Let us fill ourselves with costly wine and perfumes;
And let no flower of spring pass us by:
Let us crown ourselves with rosebuds, before they be withered:
Let none of us go without his share in our proud revelry:
Everywhere let us leave tokens of our mirth:
Because this is our portion, and our lot is this.
Let our strength be to us a law of righteousness;
For that which is weak is convicted to be of no service.'

Thus reasoned they, and they were led astray;
For their wickedness blinded them,
And they knew not the mysteries of God,
Neither hoped they for wages of holiness,
Nor did they judge that there is a prize for blameless souls.
Because God created man for incorruption,
And made him an image of His own everlastingness.
WISDOM OF SOLOMON 2. 1, 2, 4-9, 11, 21-3.

REPENTANCE OF THE
WICKED

T HEY shall say within themselves repenting:
　　'Verily we went astray from the way of truth,
We took our fill of the paths of lawlessness and destruction,
And we journeyed through trackless deserts,
But the way of the Lord we knew not.
What did our arrogancy profit us?
And what good have riches and vaunting brought us?
Those things all passed away as a shadow,
As a ship passing through the billowy water,
Whereof, when it is gone by, there is no trace to be found,
Neither pathway of its keel in the billows:
Or as when a bird flieth through the air,
No token of her passage is found,
But the light wind, lashed with the stroke of her pinions,
And rent asunder with the violent rush, is passed through by the
motion of her wings,
And afterwards no sign of her coming is found therein:
So we also, as soon as we were born, ceased to be;
And of virtue we had no sign to show,
But in our wickedness we were utterly consumed.
Because the hope of the ungodly man is as chaff carried by
the wind,

And passeth by as the remembrance of a guest that tarrieth but a day.

'But the righteous live for ever,
And in the Lord is their reward,
And the care for them with the Most High.'
WISDOM OF SOLOMON 5. 3, 6-11, 13-15.

WISE COUNSEL

I

THE soul, when accustomed to superfluous things, acquires a strong habit of desiring others which are necessary neither for the preservation of the individual nor for that of the species. This desire is without limit; whilst things which are necessary are few, and restricted within certain bounds. Lay this well to heart, reflect on it again and again; that which is superfluous is without end (and therefore the desire for it also without limit). Thus you desire to have your vessels of silver, but golden vessels are still better; others even have vessels studded with sapphires, emeralds, or rubies. Those, therefore, who are ignorant of this truth, that the desire for superfluous things is without limit, are constantly in trouble and pain. When they thus meet with the consequences of their course they complain of the judgements of God; they go so far as to say that God's power is insufficient, because He has given to this Universe the properties which they imagine cause these evils.

MOSES MAIMONIDES.

II

PREFER one in hand to two in hope; a little certainty is better than a great perhaps. Sooner a servant among the noble than leader among the common; for some of their honour will stick to you, while you must share the contempt of your contemptible followers.

The proud cedar is felled, the lowly bush is untouched; fire rises and dies away, water flows down and for ever. If for what beauty or riches you have, you raise your head above neighbour or brother, you feed hateful envy, and the beggar whom you despise may yet triumph over you. Better enough in freedom than plenty at the table of another.

Love thy children with impartial love; the hope oft errs that you place on the more promising, and all your joy may come from him that you have kept in the background.

BENEDICT OF OXFORD, 1195. (*Trans. Joseph Jacobs.*)

III

THERE are seven marks of an uncultured, and seven of a wise, man. The wise man does not speak before him who is greater than he in wisdom, and does not break in upon the speech of his fellow; he is not hasty to answer; he questions according to the subject-matter, and answers to the point; he speaks upon the first thing first, and upon the last, last; regarding that which he has not understood, he says, 'I do not understand it', and he acknowledges the truth.

ETHICS OF THE FATHERS.

THE DUTY OF HOLINESS

I AM the Lord your God: sanctify yourselves therefore, and be ye holy; for I am holy.
LEVITICUS 11. 44.

IN rabbinical ethics, holiness is the highest ideal. The entire system of the Jewish law has the hallowing of life as its aim, to be reached through good works, through observance of the Sabbath and Holydays, and through the sanctification of God's name (Kiddush Hashem). Holiness became for rabbinical Judaism synonymous with purity of life, purity of action, and purity of thought; and under its influence personal purity in Judaism became the highest standard and maxim of ethics found in any religious system.
K. KOHLER, 1904.

'CLEANLINESS is next to Godliness.'—Carefulness leads to cleanliness; cleanliness to purity; purity to humility; humility to saintliness; saintliness to fear of sin; fear of sin to holiness; and holiness to immortality.
TALMUD.

THE CITY OF GOD

D O not seek for the City of God on earth, for it is not built of wood or stone; but seek it in the soul of the man who is at peace with himself and is a lover of true wisdom.

If a man practises ablutions of the body, but defiles his mind—if he offers hecatombs, founds a temple, adorns a shrine, and does nothing for making his soul beautiful—let him not be called religious. He has wandered far from real religion, mistaking ritual for holiness; attempting, as it were, to bribe the Incorruptible and to flatter Him whom none can flatter. God welcomes the genuine service of a soul, the sacrifice of truth; but from display of wealth He turns away.

Will any man with impure soul and with no intention to repent dare to approach the Most High God? The grateful soul of the wise man is the true altar of God.

PHILO JUDAEUS, 1st cent.

THINK not meanly of thyself, and despair not of perfection.
MOSES MAIMONIDES, 1200.

A MAN should so live that at the close of every day he can repeat: 'I have not wasted my day'. ZOHAR.

HUMILITY

THE man who does good works is more likely to be overtaken by pride in them than by any other moral mischance, and its effect on conduct is injurious in the extreme. Therefore, among the most necessary of virtues is that one which banishes pride; and this is, humility.

First among the signs by which the meek are known is that when misfortunes come to them their endurance triumphs over their fear and grief, and they willingly submit to the decree of God, and own that His judgements are righteous.

In matters of justice, however, the meek will be high-spirited and fearless, punishing the wicked without fear for favour. He will help the oppressed and rescue him from the power of the oppressor.

BACHYA IBN PAKUDAH, 1040.

AT all times let a man fear God as well in private as in public, acknowledge the truth, and speak the truth in his heart; and let him rise early and say: Sovereign of all worlds! Not because of our righteous acts do we lay our supplications before Thee, but because of Thine abundant mercies.

DAILY PRAYER BOOK.

WISDOM begetteth humility.
ABRAHAM IBN EZRA, 1167.

SAYINGS FROM THE
TALMUD

I

BE thou the cursed, not he who curses. Be of them that are persecuted, not of them that persecute. Look at Scripture: there is not a single bird more persecuted than the dove; yet God has chosen her to be offered up on His altar. The bull is hunted by the lion, the sheep by the wolf, the goat by the tiger. And God said, 'Bring Me a sacrifice, not from them that persecute, but from them that are persecuted'.

Scripture ordains that the Hebrew slave who 'loves' his bondage shall have his ear pierced against the door-post (Exodus 21). Why? Because it is that ear which heard on Sinai, 'They are My servants, they shall not be sold as bondsmen'. They are *My* servants, not servants' servants. And this man voluntarily throws away his precious freedom—'Pierce his ear!'

II

EVEN when the gates of heaven are shut to prayer, they are open to tears. Prayer is Israel's only weapon, a weapon inherited from his fathers, a weapon tried in a thousand battles.

When the righteous man dies, it is the earth that loses. The lost jewel will always be a jewel, but the possessor who has lost it—well may he weep.

To one who denied resurrection, Gabiha ben Pasissa said: 'If what never before existed, exists, why may not that which once existed exist again?'

Life is a passing shadow, says Scripture. Is it the shadow of a tower, of a tree? A shadow that prevails for a while? No, it is the shadow of a bird in its flight—away flies the bird, and there is neither bird nor shadow.

Repent one day before thy death. There was a king who bade all his servants to a great repast, but did not indicate the hour. Some went home and put on their best garments and stood at the door of the palace; others said, 'There is ample time, the king will let us know beforehand'. But the king summoned them of a sudden; and those that came in their best garments were well received, but the foolish ones who came in their slovenliness, were turned away in disgrace.

Iron breaks the stone, fire melts iron, water extinguishes fire, the clouds drink up the water, a storm drives away the clouds, man withstands the storm, fear unmans man, wine dispels fear, sleep drives away wine, and death sweeps all away—even sleep. But Solomon the Wise says: 'Charity delivereth from death'.

III

FOUR shall not enter Paradise: the scoffer, the liar, the hypocrite, and the slanderer.

The cock and the owl both await the daylight. 'The light', says the cock, 'brings delight to me; but what are you waiting for?'

Thy friend has a friend, and thy friend's friend has a friend: be discreet.

He who is ashamed will not easily commit sin. Commit a sin twice, and you will think it perfectly allowable. There is a great difference between him who is ashamed before his own self, and him who is only ashamed before others.

The sun will go down all by himself, without thy assistance. Not what thou sayest about thyself, but what others say. He who humiliates himself will be lifted up; he who raises himself up will be humiliated.

Whosoever runs after greatness, greatness runs away from him; he who runs from greatness, greatness follows him.

If the young tell thee, Build; and the old tell thee, Destroy—follow the counsel of the elders; for often the destruction of the elders is construction, and the construction of the young is destruction.

IV

'FEAR God, as much as you fear man', said Johanan ben Zakkai. 'Not more?' asked his pupils in surprise. 'If you would but fear Him as much!' said the dying sage.

The righteous are masters of their passions. Not so the wicked: they are the slaves of their desires. The righteous need no monuments: their deeds are their monuments. The righteous promise little and do much; the wicked promise much and do not perform even a little. Let thy yea be yea, and thy nay be nay.

In Palestine it was considered a sign of descent from a good family if any one first broke off in a quarrel. The greatest of heroes is he who turneth an enemy into a friend.

Giving is not the essential thing, but to give with delicacy of feeling. Scripture does not say, 'Happy is he who giveth to the poor', but, 'Happy is he who *wisely considereth* the poor'. He who makes the sorrowful rejoice will partake of life everlasting.

As the ocean never freezes, so the gate of repentance is never closed. The best preacher is the heart, the best teacher time, the best book the world, the best friend God.

He who curbs his wrath, his sins will be forgiven. Whosoever does not persecute them that persecute him, whosoever takes an offence in silence, he who does good because of love, he who is cheerful under his sufferings, they are the friends of God, and of them the Scripture says, 'But they that love Him shall be as the sun, when he goeth forth in his might'.

THE DEDICATED LIFE

MOSES has shown that we should all confess our gratitude for the powers we possess. The wise man should dedicate his sagacity, the eloquent man should devote his excellence of speech, to the praise of God in prose and verse; and, in general, the natural philosopher should offer his physics, the moralist his ethics, the artist and the man of science the arts and sciences they know. So, too, the sailor and the pilot will dedicate their favourable voyage, the husbandman his fruitful harvest, the herdsman the increase of his cattle, the doctor the recovery of his patients, the general his victory in fight, and the statesman or the monarch his legal chieftaincy or kingly rule. Let no one, however humble and insignificant he be, despairing of a better fortune, scruple to become a suppliant of God. Even if he can expect nothing more, let him give thanks to the best of his power for what he has already received. Infinite are the gifts he has: birth, life, nature, soul, sensation, imagination, desire, reason. Reason is a small word, but a most perfect thing, a fragment of the world-soul, or, as for the disciples of the Mosaic philosophy it is more pious to say, a true impression of the Divine Image.

PHILO JUDAEUS, 1st cent.

GOD AND MAN

R ABBI AKIBA[1] said: Beloved is man, for he was created in the image of God; but it was by a special love that it was made known to him that he was created in the image of God.

Everything is foreseen, yet freedom of choice is given; and the world is judged by grace, yet all is according to the amount of the work.

BEN AZZAI[2] said: Despise not any man, and carp not at anything; for there is not a man that has not his hour, and there is not a thing that has not its place.

HILLEL[3] said: If I am not for myself, who will be for me? And being for myself only, what am I? and, if not now, when?

Separate not thyself from the community. Trust not in thyself until the day of thy death. Judge not thy neighbour until thou art come into his place.

ETHICS OF THE FATHERS.

1. Greatest of Mishna teachers; mystic, warrior, and martyr (132 C.E.).
2. Companion of Akiba; declared the brotherhood of man to be the fundamental principle of religion.
3. Most renowned of the Rabbis; born in Babylon about one hundred years before the Destruction of the Temple (70 C.E.).

GOLDEN RULES

T HOU shalt love thy neighbour as thyself.
    LEVITICUS 19. 18.

RABBI AKIBA said: *Thou shall love thy neighbour as thyself.* This is a fundamental principle of religion.

HILLEL used to say: *Whatever is hateful unto thee, do it not unto thy fellow.* This is the whole Law; the rest is but commentary.
    TALMUD.

'THOU shalt not hate the brother in thy heart' (Leviticus 19. 17). Our Rabbis taught that this precept might be explained to mean only that you must not injure him, nor insult him, nor vex him, and so the words *'in thine heart'* are added to forbid us even to feel hatred in our heart without giving it outward expression. Causeless hatred ranks with the three capital sins: Idolatry, Immorality, and Murder. The Second Temple, although in its time study of the Law and good works flourished and God's Commandments were obeyed, was destroyed because of causeless hatred, one of the deadly sins.

ACHAÏ (GAON), 8th cent. (*Trans. E. N. Adler.*)

DEEDS THE BEST
COMMENDATION

WHEN Akabya, son of Mahalalel, was on his death-bed, his son asked, 'Father, commend me to thy friends'. 'No, my son,' said he, 'I shall not commend thee.' 'Hast thou found aught unworthy in me?' 'No, my son,' replied he, 'thy deeds will bring thee near unto men, and thy deeds will drive thee from them.'
TALMUD.

RABBI HANINA, son of Dosa, said: He in whom the spirit of his fellow men taketh delight, in him the Spirit of the All-present taketh delight; and he in whom the spirit of his fellow men taketh not delight, in him the Spirit of the All-present taketh not delight.

RABBI JUDAH THE PRINCE said, Which is the right course that a man should choose for himself? That which he feels to be in itself honourable to the doer, and which also brings him the respect of his fellow men. Reflect upon three things, and thou wilt not come within the power of sin: Know what is above thee—a seeing Eye, a hearing Ear, and all thy deeds are written in a Book.
ETHICS OF THE FATHERS.

A MEDIAEVAL JEWISH
MORALIST

I

NO crown carries such royalty with it as doth humility; no monument gives such glory as an unsullied name; no worldly gain can equal that which comes from observing God's laws. The highest sacrifice is a broken and contrite heart; the highest wisdom is that which is found in the Law; the noblest of all ornaments is modesty; the most beautiful of all things man can do is to forgive wrong.

Cherish a good heart when thou findest it in any one; hate, for thou mayest hate it, the haughtiness of the overbearing man, and keep the boaster at a distance. There is no skill or cleverness to be compared to that which avoids temptation; there is no force, no strength that can equal piety. All honour to him who thinks continually and with an anxious heart of his Maker; who prays, reads, and learns, and all these with a passionate yearning for his Maker's grace.

II

LET thy dealings be of such sort that a blush need never visit thy cheek; be sternly dumb to the voice of passion; commit no sin, saying to thyself that thou wilt repent and make atonement at a later time. Let no oath ever pass thy lips; play not the haughty aristocrat in thine heart; follow not the desire of the eyes; banish carefully all guile from thy soul, all unseemly self-assertion from thy bearing and thy temper.

Speak never mere empty words; enter into strife with no man; place no reliance on men of mocking lips; wrangle not with evil men; cherish no too fixed good opinion of thyself, but lend thine ear to remonstrance and reproof.

Be not weakly pleased at demonstrations of honour; strive not anxiously for distinction; never let a thought of envy of those who do grave wrong cross thy mind; be never enviously jealous of others, or too eager for money.

Honour thy parents; make peace whenever thou canst among people, lead them gently into the good path; place thy trust in, give thy company to, those who fear God.

III

IF the means of thy support in life be measured out scantily to thee, remember that thou hast to be thankful and grateful even for the mere privilege to breathe, and that thou must take up that suffering as a test of thy piety and a preparation for better things. But if worldly wealth be lent to thee, exalt not thyself above thy brother; for both of ye came naked into the world, and both of ye will surely have to sleep at last together in the dust.

Bear well thy heart against the assaults of envy, which kills even sooner than death itself; and know no envy at all, save such envy of the merits of virtuous men as shall lead thee to emulate the beauty of their lives. Surrender not thyself a slave to hate, that ruin of all the heart's good resolves, that destroyer of the very savour of food, of our sleep, of all reverence in our souls.

Keep peace both within the city and without, for it goes well with all those who are counsellors of peace; be wholly sincere; mislead no one by prevarications, by words smoother than intention, as little as by direct falsehood. For God the Eternal is a God of Truth; it is He from whom truth flowed first, He who begat truth and sent it into creation.

ELEAZAR (ROKËACH) OF WORMS, *c.* 1200.

THE MYSTERY OF PAIN

THE mystery of pain is an old problem. The Rabbis were deeply impressed with its gravity and complexity. The sorrows of the universe and the agony of Israel; the suffering of the nation and the pain of the individual, formed the inspiration of some of their noblest thoughts. They fully realized that suffering can chasten and heal and purify, even 'as salt cleanses meat'. And so they call God's chastisements the blessed scourges of love, and tell us that even as the olive only gives forth its sweet and perfumed oil on being crushed, so also Israel only reaches perfection through crushing sorrows. They tell us that in the thick darkness of the world-problem is God—the 'Light Behind'; that all things work together for good—even Death; they represent God as saying to mankind, 'with thy very wounds I will heal thee'; they say that those whom God afflicts bear His name; that only through a 'sorrow's crown of sorrows' cometh true life. Heaven is not to be won by rest and ease and quiet. Only those who have suffered and endured greatly have achieved greatly. The world's greatest workers, thinkers, and teachers have only reached the pinnacle of fame by surmounting obstacles which to ordinary men, content with the lower slopes, would have seemed insuperable. Man has ever risen nearer to God by the altar-stairs of pain and sorrow—those altar-stairs which lead through darkness, for ever upwards, towards the very Throne of God.   S. ALFRED ADLER, 1906.

MEETING ADVERSITY

ACCORDING to ancient Jewish custom, the ceremony of cutting our garments when our nearest and dearest on earth is lying dead before us, is to be performed *standing up*. This teaches: meet all sorrow standing upright. The future may be dark, veiled from the eye of mortals—but not the manner in which we are to meet the future. To rail at life, to rebel against a destiny that has cast our lines in unpleasant places, is of little avail. We cannot lay down terms to life. Life must be accepted on its own terms. But hard as life's terms are, life (it has been finely said) never dictates unrighteousness, unholiness, dishonour.

J. H. HERTZ, 1900.

THE CONTEMPLATION
OF DEATH

THE contemplation of death should plant within the soul elevation and peace. Above all, it should make us see things in their true light. For all things which seem foolish in the light of death are really foolish in themselves. To be annoyed because So-and-so has slighted us or been somewhat more successful in social distinctions, pulled himself somehow one rung higher up the ladder than ourselves—how ridiculous all this seems when we couple it with the thought of death! To pass each day simply and solely in the eager pursuit of money or of fame, this also seems like living with shadows when one might take one's part with realities. Surely when death is at hand we should desire to say, 'I have contributed my grain to the great store of the eternal. I have borne my part in the struggle for goodness.' And let no man or woman suppose that the smallest social act of goodness is wasted for society at large. All our help, petty though it be, is needed; and though we know not the manner, the fruit of every faithful service is surely gathered in. Let the true and noble words of a great teacher ring in conclusion upon our ears: 'The growing good of the world is partly dependent on unhistoric acts; and that things are not so ill with you and me as they might have been, is half owing to the number who lived faithfully a hidden life and rest in unvisited tombs'.

C. G. MONTEFIORE, 1893.

REMEMBER thy last end, and cease from enmity.
ECCLESIASTICUS 28. 6.

LIGHT IN DARKNESS

W HEN Adam saw for the first time the sun go down, and an ever-deepening gloom enfold creation, his mind was filled with terror. God then took pity on him, and endowed him with the divine intuition to take two stones—the name of one was Darkness and the name of the other Shadow of Death—and rub them against each other, and so discover fire. Thereupon Adam exclaimed with grateful joy: 'Blessed be the Creator of Light'.
TALMUD.

WHENCE AND WHITHER

I

A KABYA, son of Mahalalel, said, 'Reflect upon three things, and thou wilt not come within the power of sin: know whence thou camest, and whither thou art going, and before whom thou wilt in future have to render account and reckoning'.

ETHICS OF THE FATHERS.

II

AN old Saxon chieftain was once revelling with his boon companions in the brilliantly lighted banqueting hall, when he noticed a bird flying from end to end, and he exclaimed: 'Even thus is our fate. Out of the darkness we come; we speed for a while through a gay and merry world, and then again into darkness we lapse.' Ah, not so, dear Congregants! 'The dust returneth to the earth, as it was, but the spirit returneth unto God who gave it.' Our true essence is deathless—spirit of God's undying Spirit, soul of His immortal Soul. If we have risen to a true conception of life and our duty, if we have proved ourselves faithful to our mission, then our end will not be a leap in the dark, but—

'Life's race well run,
Life's work well done,
Life's crown well won':
then come rest and peace—rest with God, peace everlasting.
HERMANN ADLER, 1898.

TIME AND ETERNITY

GOD, the Source of life, has placed in our nature the blessed hope of immortality, by which we may console ourselves for the vanity of life, and overcome the dread of death. If thou art in truth of the higher sphere, why should the thought of leaving this lower region trouble thee? Especially since the very pleasures which thou seekest on earth are, in reality, but briars and thorns. Therefore seek them not. But what shouldst thou do? This: Use thy time as thou wouldst a doubtful companion: extract the good and avoid the evil. Avail thyself of the few opportunities of improvement in his company, and use thy discretion so that thou mayest suffer no injury from thy association with him. And remember that the companionship of time is but of short duration. It flies more quickly than the shades of evening. We are like a child that grasps in his hand a sunbeam. He opens his hand soon again, but, to his amazement, finds it empty and the brightness gone.
  YEDAYA PENINI, 14th cent.

WHATSOEVER thy hand findeth to do, do it with all thy might.
  ECCLESIASTES 9. 10.

ACCUSTOM thyself to complete any good work thou hast undertaken.

DERECH ERETZ ZUTTA, 8th cent.

TALMUDIC PARABLES AND
LEGENDS

I
THE HEART ENNOBLES ANY CALLING

RABBI BAROKA, a saintly mystic, one day as he was walking through the crowded market-place of his town, met Elijah, the wandering spirit of prophecy in Jewish lore. 'Who of all this multitude has the best claim to Heaven?' asks the Rabbi of his spirit companion. The prophet points to a disreputable, weird-looking creature, a turnkey. 'That man yonder, because he is considerate to his prisoners, and refrains from all unnecessary cruelty. In that miniature hell over which he presides he has suppressed many a horror.' 'And who else is here sure of eternal life?' continues the Rabbi. Elijah then points to two motley-dressed fellows, clowns, who were supplying amusement to the bystanders. The Rabbi's astonishment knew no bounds. 'Scorn them not,' explains the prophet; 'it is always their habit, even when not performing for hire, to cheer the depressed and the sorrowful. Whenever they see a sufferer they join him, and by merry talk cause him to forget his grief.'

The heart ennobles any calling. A turnkey may leave the saintly behind in true merit of life; and a jester may be first in the kingdom of heaven, if disinterestedly he has diminished the sadness of human lives.

II
'WE LIVE IN DEEDS, NOT YEARS'

A KING had a vineyard, and he hired a number of labourers, one of whom worked more diligently and better than the others. What did the king? He took him by the hand and showed him friendship, and walked in the vineyard conversing with him. At eventide, all the labourers came to receive their hire, and the king paid that labourer too for a full day's work.

Then were the other labourers sorely vexed. They said, 'Behold, we have worked the whole day, whereas this one has only worked a few hours'.

Then said the king, 'Why do you speak thus? Consider. This one, in a few hours, did more work for me than you who toiled the whole day long.'

III
THE ACORN

A RABBI was once passing through a field where he saw a very old man planting an oak-tree. 'Why are you planting that tree?' said he. 'You surely do not expect to live long enough to see the acorn growing up into an oak-tree?'

'Ah,' replied the old man, 'my ancestors planted trees not for themselves, but for us, in order that we might enjoy their shade or their fruit. I am doing likewise for those who will come after me.'

IV
EARTHLY TREASUR

ES ALEXANDER, the world conqueror, came across a simple people in Africa who knew not war. He lingered to learn their ways. Two citizens appeared before their chief with this point of dispute: One had bought a piece of land and discovered a treasure in it; he claimed that this belonged to the seller, and wished to return it. The seller, on the other hand, declared that he sold the land with all it might contain. So he refused to accept the treasure. The chief, turning to the buyer, said: 'Thou hast a son?' 'Yes.' And addressing the seller, 'Thou hast a daughter?' 'Yes.' 'Marry one to the other and make the treasure their marriage portion.' They left content. 'In my country', said the surprised Alexander, 'the disputants would have been imprisoned, and the treasure confiscated for the king.' 'Is your country blessed by sun and rain?' asked the chief. 'Yes,' replied Alexander. 'Does it contain cattle?' 'Yes.' 'Then it must be for the sake of these innocent animals that the sun shines upon it; surely its people are unworthy of such blessing.'

V

ALEXANDER AT THE GATES OF PARADISE

ALEXANDER the Great, in his travels in the East, one day wandered to the gate of Paradise. He knocked, and the guardian angel asked, 'Who is there?' 'Alexander,' was the answer. 'Who is Alexander?' 'Alexander, you know—*the* Alexander—Alexander the Great—Conqueror of the world.' 'We know him not—he cannot enter here. *This is the Lord's gate; only the righteous enter.*' Alexander then more humbly begged for something to show he had reached the heavenly gate, and a small fragment of a human skull was thrown to him, with the words, 'Weigh it'. He took it away, and showed it contemptuously to his Wise Men, who brought a pair of scales, and, placing the bone in one, Alexander put some of his silver and gold against it in the other; but the small bone outweighed them all. More and more silver and gold were put into the scale, and at last all his crown jewels and diadems were in; but they all flew upwards like feathers before the weight of the bone, till one of the Wise Men placed a few grains of dust on the bone. Up flew the scale! The bone was that which surrounded the eye, and nothing will ever satisfy the eye until covered by the dust of the grave.

VI
HEAVENLY TREASURES

KING MONOBAZ, who in the days of the Second Temple became a proselyte to Judaism, unlocked his ancestral treasures at a time of famine, and distributed them among the poor. His ministers rebuked him, saying, 'Thy fathers amassed, thou dost squander'. 'Nay,' said the benevolent king, 'they preserved earthly, but I heavenly, treasures; theirs could be stolen, mine are beyond mortal reach; theirs were barren, mine will bear fruit time without end; they preserved money, I have preserved lives. The treasures which my fathers laid by are for this world, mine are for eternity.'

VII
TOLERATION

An aged man, whom Abraham hospitably invited to his tent, refused to join him in prayer to the one spiritual God. Learning that he was a fire-worshipper, Abraham drove him from his door. That night God appeared to Abraham in a vision and said: 'I have borne with that ignorant man for seventy years: could you not have patiently suffered him one night?'

VIII
THE TORAH IS ISRAEL'S LIFE

ONCE the Romans issued a decree that the Jews should no longer occupy themselves in the study of the Torah. Rabbi Akiba, however, was most zealous in spreading a love and knowledge of the Torah amongst all the Jewish communities. One day his friend Pappus met him and spake thus: 'Akiba, art thou not afraid? Thou surely must know that thy deeds will bring thee into mortal danger!' 'Stay a while!' retorted Akiba, 'let me tell thee a story: A fox was walking on the brink of a stream, in the clear waters of which were a number of fishes running to and fro. Said the fox to the fishes, 'Why do you run so?' 'We run', replied they, 'because we fear the fishermen's nets.' 'Come up on the dry land', said the fox, 'and live with me in safety, even as my forefathers once lived in safety with yours.' But the fishes said, 'This surely is not the cleverest amongst animals that speaks thus. Water is our natural home. If we are not safe there, how much less safe should we be on land, where we must surely die!' It is exactly so with us Jews', continued Akiba. 'The Torah is our life and the length of our days. We may, whilst loving and studying the Torah, be in great danger from our enemies; but if we were to give up its study, we should speedily disappear and be no more.'

IX
ISRAEL'S LOYALTY

THERE was once a man who betrothed himself to a beautiful maiden and then went away, and the maiden waited and he came not. Friends and rivals mocked her and said, 'He will never come'. She went into her room and took out the letters in which he had promised to be ever faithful. Weeping she read them and was comforted. In time he returned, and inquiring how she had kept her faith so long, she showed him his letters. Israel in misery, in captivity, was mocked by the nations for her hopes of redemption; but Israel went into her schools and synagogues and took out the letters, and was comforted. God would in time redeem her and say, 'How could you alone among all the mocking nations be faithful?' Then Israel would point to the Law and the Prophets and answer, 'Had I not your promise here?'

X
THE JEWELS

RABBI MEIR sat during the whole of the Sabbath-day in the School instructing the people. During his absence from the house his two sons died, both of them of uncommon beauty, and enlightened in the Law. His wife bore them to her bedchamber, and spread a white covering over their bodies. In the evening Rabbi Meir came home. 'Where are my sons?' he asked. 'I repeatedly looked round the School, and I did not see them there.' She reached him a goblet. He praised the Lord at the going out of the Sabbath, drank, and again asked: 'Where are my sons?' 'They will not be afar off', she said, and placed food before him

368

that he might eat. When he had said grace after the meal, she thus addressed him: 'With thy permission, I would fain propose to thee one question'. 'Ask it then', he replied. 'A few days ago a person entrusted some jewels into my custody, and now he demands them of me; should I give them back again?' 'This is a question', said the Rabbi, 'which my wife should not have thought it necessary to ask. What! wouldst thou hesitate to restore to every one his own?' 'No,' she replied; 'but yet I thought it best not to restore them without acquainting you therewith.' She then led him to the chamber, and took the white covering from the dead bodies. 'Ah, my sons! my sons!' loudly lamented the father. 'My sons! the light of my eyes!' The mother turned away and wept bitterly. At length she took her husband by the hand, and said: 'Didst thou not teach me that we must not be reluctant to restore that which was entrusted to our keeping? See—the Lord gave, and the Lord hath taken away; blessed be the name of the Lord!'

XI
THE TWO SHIPS

TWO ships were once seen to be sailing near land. One of them was going forth from the harbour, and the other was coming into the harbour. Every one was cheering the outgoing ship, and every one was giving it a hearty send-off. But the incoming ship was scarcely noticed.

A wise man was looking at the two ships, and he said: 'Rejoice not over the ship that is setting out to sea, for you know not what destiny awaits it, what storms it may encounter, what dangers it may have to undergo. Rejoice rather over the ship that has reached port safely and brought back all its passengers in peace.'

It is the way of the world, that when a human being is born, all rejoice; but when he dies, all sorrow. Rather ought the opposite to be the case. No one can tell what troubles await the child on its journey into manhood. But when a man has lived and dies in peace, all should rejoice, seeing that he has completed his journey, and is departing this world with the imperishable crown of a good name.

XII
THE MAN AND HIS THREE FRIENDS

A CERTAIN man had three friends, two of whom he loved dearly, but the other he lightly esteemed. It happened one day that the king commanded his presence at court, at which he was greatly alarmed, and wished to procure an advocate. Accordingly he went to the two friends whom he loved; one flatly refused to accompany him, the other offered to go with him as far as the king's gate, but no farther. In his extremity he called upon the third friend, whom he least esteemed, and he not only went willingly with him, but so ably defended him before the king that he was acquitted.

In like manner, every man has three friends when Death summons him to appear before his Creator. His first friend, whom he loves most, namely, his money, cannot go with him a single step; his second, relations and neighbours, can only accompany him to the grave, but cannot defend him before the Judge; while his third friend, whom he does not highly esteem—his good works—goes with him before the King, and obtains his acquittal.

XIII
VANITY OF HUMAN PLEASURE

A FOX was eyeing longingly some luscious fruit in a very fine garden. But there was no way for him to enter. At last he espied an opening through which, he thought, he might possibly get in, but soon found the hole too small to admit his body. 'True,' he said, 'the hole is small, but if I fast three days my body will become sufficiently reduced to admit me.' He did so; and to his joy he now feasted to his heart's content upon the grapes and all the other good things in the orchard. But lo! when he desired to escape before the master of the garden came upon him he saw, to his great consternation, that the opening had again become too small for him. Poor animal! he had a second time to fast three days; and having made good his escape, he cast a farewell glance upon the scene of his late revels, saying: 'O garden, charming art thou and exquisite are thy fruits! But of what avail hast thou been unto me? What have I now for all my labour and cunning?'

It is even so with man. Naked he comes into the world, naked he must leave it. Of all his toil therein he carries nothing away with him save the fruits of his good deeds.

XIV
BODY AND SOUL

THE Roman Emperor Antoninus once said to Rabbi Judah the Prince, 'On the great Day of Judgement, soul and body will each plead excuse for sin committed. The body will say to the Heavenly Judge, "It is the soul, and not I, that has sinned. Without it I am as lifeless as a stone." On the other hand, the soul will say, "How canst Thou impute sin to me? It is the body that has dragged me down."'

'Let me tell you a parable', answered Rabbi Judah the Prince. 'A king once had a beautiful garden stocked with the choicest fruits. He set two men to keep guard over it—a blind man and a lame man. "I see some fine fruit yonder", said the lame man one day. "Come up on my shoulder", said the blind man, "I will carry you to the spot, and we shall both enjoy the fruit." The owner, missing the fruit, haled both men before him for punishment. "How could I have been the thief?" queried the lame man, "seeing that I cannot walk?" "Could I have stolen the fruit?" retorted the blind man; "I am unable to see anything." What did the king? He placed the lame man on the shoulders of the blind man and sentenced them both as one.'

In the same way will the Divine Judge of the Universe mete out judgement to body and soul jointly.

ALMIGHTY, WHAT IS MAN?

A LMIGHTY! what is man?
　　But flesh and blood.
Like shadows flee his days,
He marks not how they vanish from his gaze,
Now like a flower blowing,
Now scorched by sunbeams glowing.
And wilt Thou of his trespasses inquire?
How may he ever bear
Thine anger just, Thy vengeance dire?
Then spare him, be Thou merciful, O King,
Upon the dreaded day of reckoning!
Almighty! what is man?
A faded leaf!
If Thou dost weigh him in the balance—lo!
He disappears—a breath that thou dost blow.
His heart is ever filled
With lust of lies unstilled.
Wilt Thou bear in mind his crime
Unto all time?
He fades away like clouds sun-kissed,
Dissolves like mist.

Then spare him! let him love and mercy win,
According to Thy grace, and not according to his sin!
SOLOMON IBN GABIROL, 1050. (*Trans. Emma Lazarus.*)

RESIGNATION

R IGHTEOUS art Thou, O God, and ever just,
     And none can question, none withstand Thy will;
And though our hearts be humbled to the dust,
Teach us, through all, to see Thy mercy still.
Our life is measured out by Thee above,
And to Thy will each human heart must bow;
No frail remonstrance mars our perfect love,
No man shall say to Thee, 'What doest Thou?'
When suffering to human fault is due,
Forgive, O Lord, and stay Thine hand, we pray;
And when it brings but trial of faith anew,
Turn Thou the night of gloom to trustful day.
When blessings bring Thy sunshine to our heart,
Let gratitude uplift each soul at rest;
And when to bear our griefs becomes our part,
Let faith and hope exhort us—God knows best.
The Lord hath given—praise unto His Name!
But with that praise our task is but begun.
The Lord hath taken—still our thought the same,
His is Law our Law; His will, not ours, be done.
A. A. GREEN, 1917.

IMMORTALITY

THERE are those who gain eternity in a lifetime, others who gain it in one brief hour.

TALMUD.

RABBI JACOB[1] said: This world is like a vestibule before the world to come. Prepare thyself in the vestibule, so that thou mayest enter into the palace.

Better is one hour of repentance and good deeds in this world than the whole life in the world to come; and better is one hour of blissfulness of spirit in the world to come than the whole life of this world.

ETHICS OF THE FATHERS.

---

1. Mishna teacher of the 2nd century.

ETERNAL HOPE

W HOM have I in heaven but Thee?
     And there is none upon earth that I desire beside Thee.
My flesh and my heart faileth:
But God is the strength of my heart and my portion for ever.
PSALM 73. 25-6.

TRUE WISDOM

S URELY there is a mine for silver,
    And a place for gold which they refine.
Iron is taken out of the earth,
And brass is molten out of the stone.
Man setteth an end to darkness,
And searcheth out to the farthest bound
The stones of thick darkness and of the shadow of death.
He breaketh open a shaft away from where men sojourn;
He putteth forth his hand upon the flinty rock;
He overturneth the mountains by the roots.
He cutteth out passages among the rocks,
And his eye seeth every precious thing.
He bindeth the streams that they trickle not,
And the thing that is hid bringeth he forth to light.
But where shall wisdom be found?
And where is the place of understanding?
Man knoweth not the price thereof;
Neither is it found in the land of the living.
The deep saith, It is not in me:
And the sea saith, It is not with me.
It cannot be gotten for gold,
Neither shall silver be weighed for the price thereof.

Whence then cometh wisdom?
And where is the place of understanding?
Destruction and Death say,
We have heard a rumour thereof with our ears,
God understandeth the way thereof,
And He knoweth the place thereof,
And unto man He said,
Behold, the fear of the Lord, that is wisdom;
And to depart from evil is understanding.
JOB 28. 1–4, 9–15, 20, 22–3, 28.

RABBI TARPHON[1] said: The day is short, and the work is great, but the labourers are idle, though the reward be great, and the Master of the work is urgent. It is not incumbent upon thee to complete the work; but neither art thou free to desist from it. Faithful is thine Employer to pay the reward of thy labour. But know that the reward unto the righteous is not of this world.
ETHICS OF THE FATHERS.

REMEMBER also thy Creator in the days of thy youth, or ever the evil days come, and the years draw nigh, when thou shalt say, I have no pleasure in them: or ever the sun and the light, and the moon and the stars be darkened, and the clouds return after the rain; and the dust return to the earth as it was, and the spirit return to God who gave it.

This is the end of the matter; all hath been heard: fear God, and keep His commandments, for this is the whole duty of man.
ECCLESIASTES 12. 1–2, 7, 13.

---

1. Mishna teacher of the 2nd century.

NOTES

T HROUGHOUT this Jewish Anthology the unit of selection is the Jewish *thought*. Abridgement has therefore been unhesitatingly resorted to wherever condensation helped to make the thought stand out in clearer light. Utmost care has, however, been taken that such condensation in no way obscures the original meaning of the Author.

The bibliographic notes are intended for those who may desire to extend their acquaintance with Jewish books. Only such sources as are available in English and are within possible reach of the ordinary reader have been indicated.

In the Scripture selections, wherever the rhythm and beauty of either the Authorized Version or the Revised Version could be retained, this has been done. In the majority of cases, however, the quotations are from the more faithful Jewish Version. The numbering of the Bible verses is according to the Hebrew text.

ABBREVIATIONS:

- J. Q. R. = Jewish Quarterly Review (Old Series).
- J. P. S. = Jewish Publication Society of America, Philadelphia.
- J. E. = Jewish Encyclopedia. This standard reference work should be consulted for fuller information on the authors, sources, and subjects brought together in this book.

I

-Jacobs: 'The Typical Character of Anglo-Jewry,' J. Q. R., 1898.

-Aguilar: *The Spirit of Judaism*, chap. VIII. A. S. Isaacs' *The Young Champion* is a biography of Grace Aguilar for young readers. J. P. S., 1916.

-For Eleazar of Worms, see M. Joseph in *Jews' College Jubilee Volume*, 1905.

-Montefiore: From a Sermon preached before the Jewish students of Cambridge University.

'Individual offences bring shame not only upon the persons who commit them, but upon the entire race, which, says an old writer, like a harp-string, has but to be struck at one end and it vibrates throughout. This has been the fate of Israel in every age; and the world's habit of identifying the race with the shortcomings of the individual seems to be ineradicable. Public transgression—transgression which involves the whole House of Israel—is in a special sense branded as a *Chillul Hashem*, as "a profanation of the Name" just as good deeds, done publicly, which reflect lustre on all Israel, are praised as a *Kiddush Hashem*, "a sanctification of the Name".' (Morris Joseph, *Judaism as Life and Creed*. 3rd Edition. Routledge—an excellent book that should be in every English-speaking Jewish home.)

-For other specimens of Jewish Moralists see *Hebrew Characteristics*, published by the old American Jewish Publication Society, 1872; and I. Abrahams, 'Jewish Ethical Wills,' in J. Q. R., 1891.

-Philipson: *Old European Jewries*, J. P. S.

-Lazarus: Quoted in Nahida Remy, *The Jewish Woman*. (Bloch Publishing Co., New York.)

-The Jewish Home—Cf. Morris Joseph on the question of inter-marriage.

'Every Jew should feel himself bound, even though the duty involves the sacrifice of precious affections, to avoid acts calculated, however remotely, to weaken the stability of the ancestral religion. It is true that occasional unions between Jew and Gentile do no appreciable harm to the Jewish cause, however much mischief they may lay up, in the shape of jealousy and dissension, for those who contract them, and of religious confusion, for the children. But a general practice begins as a rule by being occasional. Every Jew who contemplates marriage outside the pale must regard himself as paving the way to a disruption which will be the final, as it will be the culminating, disaster in the history of his people.'

-Szold: 'What has Judaism done for Woman?' in *Judaism at the* [Chicago] *World's Parliament of Religions*, Cincinnati, 1894.

-Cradle Song: quoted in Schechter, *Studies in Judaism*, i, 1896. 'The Child in Jewish Literature.' Another version in I. Zangwill's *They that Walk in Darkness* is as follows:—

Sleep, my birdie, shut your eyes,
Oh, sleep, my little one;
Too soon from cradle you'll arise
To work that must be done.
Almonds and raisins you shall sell,
And Holy Scrolls shall write;
So sleep, dear child, sleep sound and well,
Your future beckons bright.
Brum shall learn of ancient days,
And love good folk of this;
So sleep, dear babe, your mother prays,
And God will send you bliss.

-For the Yiddish folk-song see Wiener, *History of Yiddish Literature in the Nineteenth Century*, New York and London, 1899; and Kurt Schindler, 'The Russian-Jewish Folk Song', in *The Menorah Journal*, New York, 1917.

-'The Russian Jewish folk-song has grown and was reared under the greatest oppression, and the grimmest tyranny that a race ever went through. By this very oppression it has become tense, quivering, abounding with emotion; in its melodies the Jewish heart is laid open, and it speaks in a language understandable to all. Its songs have an elemental appeal—they represent the collective outcry of a suffering, unbendable race.' (Schindler.)

-Cohen: Preface, *Children's Psalm Book*. (Routledge.)

-The following words recently written by America's leading educationist are of deep significance—'Education the world over was at first for a long time almost solely religious, and, while it was once a masterstroke of toleration to eliminate it from the school, in doing so we nearly lost from our educational system the greatest of all the motives that makes for virtue, reverence, self-knowledge and self-control. Now we are beginning to realize the wrong we have committed against child-nature and are seeking in various ways to atone for it.' (G. Stanley Hall, in Introduction to L. Grossmann's *The Aims of Teaching in Jewish Schools*, Cincinnati, 1919.)

-Cf. the chapter on Religious Education with Bibliography in M. Friedländer, *The Jewish Religion*, second edition (P. Vallentine).

-Morais: in *Abarbanel's School and Family Reader for Israelites*, New York, 1883, a book well worth reprinting.

-Joseph, *The Message of Judaism* (G. Routledge), 'Hebrew and the Synagogue.'

-Schechter: *Seminary Addresses*, Ark Publishing Co., Cincinnati, 1915. These addresses of eloquent wisdom contain the ripest thoughts of that great scholar.

-In 1870 Peretz Smolenskin, then the foremost neo-Hebrew writer, proclaimed: 'The wilfully blind bid us be like all the other nations. Yea, let us be like all the other nations, unashamed of the rock whence we have been hewn; like the rest, holding dear our language and the honour of our people. We need not blush for clinging to the ancient language with which we wandered from land to land, in which our poets sang, and our seers prophesied, and in which our fathers poured out their hearts unto God. They who thrust us away from the Hebrew language meditate evil against our people and against its glory.'

-Maimonides: Some scholars question the Maimonidean authorship of this Admonition.

-In *Year Book of Central Conference of American Rabbis*, 1904.

-*Aspects of Rabbinic Theology*, p. 76.

-Adler: *Anglo-Jewish Memories*, p. 272.

-Gabirol: Probably the very earliest enunciation of Tolerance in Western Europe.

-*Against Apion*, concluding paragraphs.

Ecclesiasticus: Written originally in Hebrew by Simon ben Jeshua ben Sira, who flourished in Jerusalem in the second century, B.C.E. Translated into Greek by the author's grandson, who resided in Egypt between 132–116. The Hebrew original was lost for over 1,000 years, and was re-discovered in the Cairo Geniza by Dr. Schechter in 1896.

-The change from the Revised Version in the second line is according to the newly-discovered Hebrew original.

-*Their name liveth for evermore*; the phrasing of the Authorized Version has been restored. These five words have been chosen by the Imperial War Graves Commission as the inscription for the central monuments on the cemeteries in France and Flanders.

-Dubnow: *Jewish History*, J. P. S., chap. 12. Dubnow's sketch is a brief, philosophical survey of Jewish History.

-Hertz: From Presidential Address, Union of Jewish Literary Societies, 'On "Renaissance" and "Culture" and their Jewish Applications'.

-Geiger: *Judaism and its History*, I, 2.

-*Aspects of Rabbinic Theology*, p. 112.

-*Jews in Many Lands*. J. P. S.

-Singer: *Sermons*, I. 'Judaism and Citizenship.' (Routledge.)

-Achad Ha'am: *Selected Essays*, J. P. S., 1912. 'Some Consolation.' A number of those original and thought-compelling essays have been republished in the series *Zionist Pamphlets*, 1916 & 1917.

-The words 'The Duty of Self-Respect' are the title of a paper by the late F. D. Mocatta.

-Nordau: Address at First Zionist Congress, Basle.

-Schechter: *Seminary Addresses*. 'Higher Criticism—Higher Anti-Semitism.'

-Disraeli: From Preface to *Collected Works of Isaac D'Israeli*.

-Hertz: From Reply to 'Verax', *The Times*, November 29, 1919.

-Recent anti-Semitic attacks in the Press recall Steinschneider's comment: 'When dealing with Jewish questions it is not necessary to be either logical or fair. It seems one may say anything of Jews so long as it brings them into contempt.'

-*An Epistle to the Hebrews*. Letter 4. Republished by the Federation of American Zionists, 1900.

-These stirring lines were written during the Boer War.

-Dr. Adler continues: 'Here we are spared the most distressful sight, the revival of odious religious prejudices and pernicious racial antipathies.' These words would require some qualification to-day.

-*Songs of a Wanderer*, J. P. S.

-'Why am I a Jew?' North American Review.

-A similar thought is expressed by the same writer in his Address at the Chicago Parliament of Religions: 'There is a legend that when Adam and Eve were turned out of Eden, an angel shattered the gates, and the fragments flying all over the earth are the precious stones. We can carry the legend further. The precious stones were picked up by the various religions and philosophies of the world. Each claimed and claims that its own fragment alone reflects the light of heaven. In God's own time we shall, all of us, fit our fragments together and reconstruct the Gates of Paradise. Through the gates shall all peoples pass to the foot of God's throne. The throne is called by us the mercy-seat. Name of happy augury, for God's Mercy shall wipe out all record of mankind's errors and strayings, the sad story of our unbrotherly actions.'

-*Judaism as Creed and Life.* Book III, chap. X. Book III is the best modern presentation of the ethical life under the aspect of Judaism.

II

-Lucas: *The Jewish Year*, Macmillan, 1898. Every one of Mrs. Lucas's admirable versions of the principal mediaeval Jewish hymns quoted in this book are from the above volume.

-Levi: See Miss Helen Zimmern's monograph on 'David Levi, Poet and Patriot', in the J. Q. R., 1897.

-Zangwill: 'The Position of Judaism'. North American Review.

-Schechter: *Seminary Addresses*. 'Higher Criticism—Higher Anti-Semitism'.

-Sulzberger: From Address at the Decennial Meeting of the J. P. S.

-Leeser: Preface, *The Twenty-four Books of the Holy Scriptures*.

-Adler: From a Sermon, 'This Book of the Law'.

-Rashi: On Exodus vi. 9. *Scripture must be interpreted according to its plain, natural sense*—an epoch-making pronouncement in the history of Bible exegesis. Though he is not the author of this canon of interpretation, Rashi is the first seriously to attempt its application. 'Rashi deserves the foremost place which the judgment of Jewish scholars generally accords him. He has two of the greatest and rarest gifts of the commentator, the instinct to discern precisely the point at which explanation is necessary, and the art of giving or indicating the needed help in the fewest words.' (G. F. Moore.)

-Halevi: *Cusari*, II, 56. Translated by H. Hirschfeld under the Arabic title *Kitab Al-Khazari* (Routledge), 1905.

-Geiger: *Judaism and its History*, I, 3.

-Jacobs: *Jewish Contributions to Civilization*, J. P. S.

-Shemtob: A remarkable anticipation by over three and a half centuries of the modern view of the rôle of the Prophets.

-Compare with the two other selections on the Prophets the following by Felix Adler:—

'Either we must place nature uppermost, or man uppermost. If we choose the former, then man himself becomes a mere soulless tool in the hands of destiny, a part of a machine, the product of his circumstances. If we choose the latter, then all nature will catch a reflected light from the glory of the moral aims of man.

'The Hebrew Prophets chose the latter alternative. They asserted the freedom of man; and the general conscience of mankind, despite all cavilings and sophistry to the contrary, has ever responded to their declaration with a loud Amen. They argued, to put their thought in modern language, that we may fairly judge of the whole course of evolution by its highest outcome, and they believed its highest outcome to be, not mere mechanical order of beauty, but righteousness.

'The Hebrew Prophets interpreted the universe in terms of humanity's aspirations. They believe that the ends of justice are too precious to be lost; that, if righteousness is not yet real in the world, it must be made real; and, hence, that there must be a Power in the world which makes for righteousness.'

-Darmesteter: *Selected Essays*, translated by Jastrow, N. Y., 1895.

-Lazarus: *The Spirit of Judaism*, New York, 1895.

-*The Literary Remains of Emanuel Deutsch*, 1874. *The Talmud: Two Essays by Deutsch and Darmesteter*, J. P. S., 1911.

-*Chapters in Jewish Literature*, J. P. S. Preface.

-Magnus: *Outlines of Jewish History*, J. P. S., p. 333.

-Jacobs: *Jewish Ideals and other Essays*, 1896.

-Halevi: *Cusari*, II, 36.

-Gaster: Presidential Address, Transactions of Jewish Historical Society of England, vol. VII.

-*Jewish History*, concluding paragraph.

-Zunz: *Synagogale Poesie des Mittelalters*, chap. ii. 'Leiden.' This wonderful presentation of the Sufferings of the Jews in the Middle Ages has been translated by Dr. A. Löwy in *Miscellany of Hebrew Literature*. First Series, 1872; and has been republished in the 'Library of Jewish Classics', Bloch Publishing Co., New York, 1916.

-*Antiquities of the Jews*. Book XVIII, 8.

-Dean Plumptre, *Lazarus and other Poems*.

-Heine: The following is a more literal version by Nina Salaman:—

Break out in loud lamenting,
Thou sombre martyr-song,
That all aflame I have carried
In my silent soul so long.
Into all ears it presses,
Thence every heart to gain—
I have conjured up so fiercely
The thousand-year-old pain.
The great and small are weeping,
Even men so cold of eye;
The women weep and the flowers,
The stars are weeping on high.
And all these tears are flowing
In silent brotherhood,
Southward-flowing and falling
All into Jordan's flood.

-*Curiosities of Literature*, vol. II.

-Abarbanel's *Reader*.

-*Poems of Emma Lazarus, New York*, 1889, vol. II.

-*Songs of Exile*, J. P. S., 1901.

-From 'Jewish Ethics' (M. Joseph) in *Religious Systems of the World*, London, 1892.

-'Vindiciae Judaeorum', I. 7, in L. Wolf, *Manasseh Ben Israel's Mission to Oliver Cromwell*, 1901.

-Hirsch: *Nineteen Letters of Ben Uziel*, 16th Letter (Funk and Wagnalls) New York, 1899.

-J. E., vol. XII, 348.

-Hertz: 'Lord Rothschild: A Memorial Sermon.'

-*History of the Jews in Poland and Russia* (Putnams), 1915, conclusion.

-*Past and Present: A Collection of Jewish Essays*, chap. XVI, Ark Publishing Co., Cincinnati, 1919.

-'What is a pogrom? Better than any abstract definition is a concrete record taken haphazard of an actual pogrom. Orscha is a town of 14,000 inhabitants, half of them Jews. On October 18, 1905, the news of the proclamation of the Constitution reached Orscha. On the 19th the general strike stopped; Jew and Christian embraced; the houses were hung with flags, a service of thanksgiving was held; processions filled the streets. In the evening the Mohilev police officer Misgaib entered the town, and the rumour ran round that a patriotic demonstration was to take place and the Jews to be beaten. On the 20th, drunken men gathered to take the official's orders. On the morning of the 21st, the peasants entered the town armed with axes and guns. "The village authorities have sent us; whoever does not come will be punished. We are to do whatever is ordered." At one o'clock a priest exhorted the crowds of the faithful to purge their city of the aliens, and the cry arose, "Long live absolutism! Down with the mayor, who has sold the town to the Jews". The first murders followed. The house of a rich Jew was stormed. Without the soldiers fired, a priest held service, and a band played the national anthem; while within eight men, women and children were tortured to death. The appetite was only whetted. At six o'clock the peasants begged the police for more orders, more work. They were told to wait till daylight; the darkness might encourage the Jews to resist. On the same day twelve Jewish youths came from Shklov to help their brethren. They were met at the station and murdered, and for seven hours every man that passed mutilated or insulted their dead bodies. The massacre became general. The 23rd was given up to plunder. At mid-day the Vice-Governor spoke to the crowds: "Children, it is enough. You have had three days' amusement, now go home and sing 'God save the Czar'". The pogrom at Orscha was typical of the 690 greater and lesser pogroms which took place that October.' (H. Sacher on 'Die Judenpogromme in Russland'. *Jewish Review*, i.)

-Wolf: '*The Legal Sufferings of the Jews in Russia.*'

-Lazarus: First appeared in '*Songs of a Semite*', New York, 1882.

Each crime that wakes in man the beast,
Is visited upon his kind.

The lines, written in 1882, apply with hundredfold force to the uninterrupted pogroms that have been raging in the Ukraine throughout 1919. More than 100,000 Jews—men, women, and children—have been butchered in cold blood by the hordes under Generals Denikin and Petlura. The soldiery, intoxicated with blood, invented the most diabolical tortures. See the Report on Jewish Pogroms by Kieff Pogrom Relief Committee, controlled by the Russian Red Cross, London, 1920. 'Our masses in Eastern Europe have been facing death in seven circles of hell. It is sufficient to remember the multi-massacres of Ukrainia. For this cold murder of whole communities not Heaven itself nor all the mercy of the angels could find palliation. There is no instance that shows so much as this the ghastly descent of human character into primitive brutality and cannibalism. This is a deed which in its horror and wicked purposelessness should have stunned the world.' (Nahum Sokolow, Opening Address of London Zionist Conference, July 7, 1920.) The following stanzas are from Mr. Zangwill's appeal to American Jewry on behalf of the victims:—

OUR OWN

By devastated dwellings,
By desecrated fanes,
By hearth-stones, cold and crimsoned,
And slaughter-reeking lanes,
Again is the Hebrew quarter
Through half of Europe known;
And crouching in the shambles,
Rachel, the ancient crone,
Weeps again for her children and the fate that is her own.
No laughter rings in these ruins
Save of girls to madness shamed.
Their mothers disembowelled
Lie stark 'mid children maimed.
The Shool has a great congregation
But never a psalm they drone.
Shrouded in red-striped Tallisim,
Levi huddles with Kohn;
But the blood from their bodies oozing is the blood that is
    your own.
Shot, some six to the bullet,
Lashed and trailed in the dust,
Mutilated with hatchets
In superbestial lust—
No beast can even imagine

What Christians do or condone—
Surely these bear our burden
And for our sins atone,
And if we hide our faces, then the guilt is as our own.
At last but a naked rabble,
Clawing the dust for bread,
Jabbering, wailing, whining,
Hordes of the living dead,
Half apes, half ghosts, they grovel,
Nor human is their tone,
Yet they are not brutes but brethren,
These wrecks of the hunger-zone,
And their death-cry rings to heaven in the tongue that is
    your own.

-For an historical account of these child-martyrdoms, see Dubnow, *History of the Jewish Russia and Poland*, J. P. S., 1918, vol. ii, pp. 18-29.

-*Stories and Pictures*, J. P. S., 1906, contains the best work of Peretz. The Yiddish original of 'Bontzie Schweig', with English translation, is published in Wiener, pp. 332-53.

With Peretz, Yiddish letters 'enter into competition with what is best in the world's literature, where he will some day occupy an honourable place. Peretz offers gladly all he has, his genius, in the service of the lowly. Literature, according to him, is a consolation to those who have no other consolation, a safe and pleasurable retreat for those who are buffeted about on the stormy sea of life. For these reasons he prefers to dwell with the down-trodden and the submerged.' (Wiener).

-Cf. Emma Lazarus' *Banner of the Jew*:—

Oh for Jerusalem's trumpet now,
To blow a blast of shattering power,
To wake the sleepers high and low,
And rouse them to the urgent hour!
No hand for vengeance—but to save,
A million naked swords should wave.
Oh deem not dead that martial fire,
Say not the mystic flame is spent!
With Moses' law and David's lyre,

Your ancient strength remains unbent.
Let but an Ezra rise anew,
To lift the *Banner of the Jew*!
A rag, a mock at first—ere long,
When men have bled and women wept
To guard its precious folds from wrong,
Even they who shrunk, even they who slept,
Shall leap to bless it, and to save.
Strike! for the brave revere the brave!

'When the anti-Semite agitation took the form of massacre and spoliation, several pamphlets were published by Jews in Russia, advocating the restoration of the Jewish State. They found a powerful echo in the United States, where a young Jewish poetess, Miss Emma Lazarus, passionately championed the Zionist cause in verse not unworthy of Yehudah Halevi.' (Lucien Wolf, *Encyclopaedia Britannica*, 'Zionism'.)

-*Seminary Addresses*, 'Zionism'.

-*Selected Essays*, 'Moses'.

-*Jewish Review*, I.

-Herzl: 'Herzl's personal charm was irresistible. His sincerity, his eloquence, his tact, his devotion, his power, were recognized on all hands. He spent his whole strength in the furtherance of his ideas. Diplomatic interviews, exhausting journeys, impressive mass meetings, brilliant literary propaganda—all these methods were employed by him to the utmost limit of self-denial. He was beyond question the most influential Jewish personality of the nineteenth century. He effectively roused Jews all the world over to an earnest and vital interest in their present and their future. Herzl thus left an indelible mark on his time, and his renown is assured whatever be the fate in store for the political Zionism which he founded and for which he gave his life.' (I. Abrahams in *Encyclopaedia Britannica*.)

-Herzl: Address at Zionist Congress, London, 1900.

-Hertz: Address at Thanksgiving Meeting for the Balfour Declaration, Dec. 2, 1917.

-Herzl: Address at First Zionist Congress, Basle, 1897.

-Schechter: *Aspects*, 105.

-Noah: See 'Noah's Ark' in Zangwill's *Dreamers of the Ghetto* for an account of this early American Zionist.

III

-Cornill: In the same masterly address, *Humanity in the Old Testament,* this great Biblical scholar says:—

'But not only to man does the humanitarianism of the Torah extend, it cares for the brute as well, and places it likewise under legal protection, to which I know of no analogy in older extra-Israelitish codes. The Israelite ascribed a soul even to the brute, and saw in it a creature of God, which, while subservient to man by God, yet should not be helplessly exposed to his caprice. What a truly humanitarian sentiment finds expression in the Law; "Thou shalt not muzzle the ox when he treadeth out the corn". The brute should not perform hard labour, and at the same time have food before its eyes, without the possibility of eating therefrom. I remember some time ago, to have read that one of the richest Italian real-estate owners, at the grape-harvest, fastened iron muzzles to his miserable, fever-stricken work-men, so that it might not occur to these poor peasants, working for star-vation wages under the glowing sun of Southern Italy, to satiate their burning thirst and their gnawing hunger with a few of the millions of grapes of the owner.'

-*Literature and Dogma,* 1, 4, and XI, 6.

-*History of the People of Israel.* Preface.

-Lotze: *Microcosm,* III.

-Frazer: *Passages of the Bible chosen for their Literary Beauty.*

—Preface.

Compare the following from the same writer's *The Folklore of the Old Testament* (Macmillan, 1918):—

'The revelation of the baser elements which underlay the civiliza-tion of ancient Israel, as they underlie the civilization of modern Europe, serves rather as a foil to enhance by contrast the glory of a people which, from such dark depths of ignorance and cruelty, could rise to such bright heights of wisdom and virtue. The annals of sava-gery and superstition unhappily compose a large part of human litera-ture; but in what other volume shall we find, side by side with that melancholy record, psalmists who poured forth their sweet and solemn strains of meditative piety in the solitude of the hills or in green pastures and beside still waters; prophets who lit up their beatific visions of a blissful future with the glow of an impassioned imagination; historians who bequeathed to distant ages the scenes of a remote past embalmed for ever in the amber of a pellucid style? These are the true glories of the Old Testament and of Israel.'

-Huxley: *Educational Essays.*

-Huxley: 'From the free spirit of the Mosaic law sprang the intensity of family life that amid all dispersions and persecutions has preserved the individuality of the Hebrew race; that love of independence that under the most adverse circumstance has characterized the Jew; that burning patriotism that flamed up in the Maccabees and bared the breasts of Jewish peasants to the serried steel of Grecian phalanx and the resistless onset of Roman legion; that stubborn courage that in exile and in torture held the Jew to his faith. It kindled that fire that has made the strains of Hebrew seers and poets phrase for us the highest exaltations of thought; that intellectual vigour that has over and over again made the dry staff bud and blossom. And it has exerted its power wherever the influence of the Hebrew scriptures has been felt. It has toppled thrones and cast down hierarchies.' (Henry George.)

-Renan: *History of the People of Israel*, chap. 7.

-*Moses.* This splendid lecture should be read in full. It is published in a penny edition by the 'Land Value' Publication Dept., Strand.

-Dow: 'Hebrew and Puritan', J. Q. R., III.

-Rhys: *Lyrical Poetry from the Bible.* (Dent.) Introduction.

-Cornill: *The Culture of Ancient Israel.* Open Court Publishing Co., Chicago. 'The Psalms in the World's Literature.'

-Jowett: *Selected Passages from the Theological Writings*, 1903, p. 53.

-*The Prophets of Israel.* Open Court Publishing Co., Chicago, 1895.

-Stanley: *History of the Jewish Church*, III, lecture 45.

-'Social Life in France in the Fourteenth Century' (The Jews), Fortnightly Review, vol. 57.

-*The Shield*, edited by Gorky, &c., A. A. Knopf, New York, 1917. 'Russia and the Jews.'

-Herford: *Pharisaism: Its aim and methods*, 1912, chap. VI.

-'A Theist's Impressions of Judaism', J. Q. R., XIX.

-*Israel among the Nations.* New York, 1893.

-*Rationalism in Europe*, chap. VI.

-*Short History of the English People*, chap. VIII, I.

-*Essay and Speech on Jewish Disabilities*, ed. I. Abrahams and S. Levy. (Jewish Historical Society of England) 1910.

-From 'A Letter on the Jew' sent to a Jewish meeting, Capetown, July 1, 1906.

-Milyukov: In *The Shield*, 'The Jewish Question in Russia'.

-Lecky: *Democracy and Liberty*, 1896.

-The Talmudic Story is from *Three Legends* (Berlin, 1904), written and published by Tolstoy in aid of the victims of the Kishineff pogrom.

-Schreiner: See Note.

-The British Protest, together with the French, German, and Russian Protests, were republished in pamphlet form by the *Jewish Chronicle* in 1913.

-Quoted in Davies's *Gems from the Fathers* (Bagster).

IV

-Philo: C. G. Montefiore, 'Florilegium Philonis', in J. Q. R. VII (1895) is a good introduction to the Moses Mendelssohn of Hellenistic Judaism.

-Abrahams: *Authorized Prayer Book, Annotated Edition*, p. VIII.

-Both Mrs. Lucas in *The Jewish Year*, and Mr. Zangwill in *The Service of the Synagogue* (Routledge) have produced versions of Adon Olam. The following is by George Borrow in *The Bible in Spain*:—

Reigned the Universe's Master, ere were earthly things begun;
When His mandate all created, Ruler was the name he won;
And alone He'll rule tremendous when all things are past
    and gone,
He no equal has, nor consort, He, the singular and lone,
Has no end and no beginning; His the sceptre, might, and
    throne.
He's my God and living Saviour, rock to whom in need I run;
He's my banner and my refuge, fount of weal when call'd
    upon;
In His hand I place my spirit, at nightfall and at rise of sun,
And therewith my body also; God's my God—I fear no one.

-From the first Jewish Hymn Book in America—a free rendering.

-*The Menorah Journal*, vol. II, 1916. 'A Plea for Orthodoxy.'

-Hertz: *Inaugural Sermon*, Congregation Orach Chayim, New York, 1912.

-Abrahams: 'Judaism and Spiritism', in *Jewish Guardian*, October 1, 1919.

-In Philipson, *Old European Jewries*, J. P. S.

-Jacobs: *Jewish Ideals*. 'And what great bliss and happiness did the Sabbath bring to the family life. When Friday evening came and the Sabbath lamps were lighted and our fathers sang their Sabbath hymns, they forgot, once in each week, all the sorrows and cares of everyday life, and all the affronts and insults which, without pity and without mercy, were heaped upon them, and at last on the Sabbath they felt released in body and soul from all troubles and burdens.' (B. Felsenthal.)

A SABBATH TABLE-SONG.
Treasure of heart for the broken people,
Gift of new soul for the souls distrest,
Soother of sighs for the prisoned spirit—
The Sabbath of rest.
This day is for Israel light and rejoicing,
A Sabbath of rest.
When the work of the worlds in their wonder was finished,
Thou madest this day to be holy and blest,
And those heavy-laden find safety and stillness,
A Sabbath of rest.
This day is for Israel light and rejoicing,
A Sabbath of rest.
ISAAC LURIA, 1560. (*Trans. Nina Salaman.*)

-*Songs of a Wanderer.*

-See *Authorized Prayer Book, Annotated Edition*, pp. cxlix and cclix.

-Also in *Songs of a Wanderer.*

-*The Ideal in Judaism*, 1893.

-Hertz: Passover as Israel's birthday. 'A people who, though they never founded a great empire nor built a great metropolis, have exercised upon a large portion of mankind an influence, wide-spread, potent and continuous; a people who have for nearly two thousand years been without country or organized nationality yet have preserved their identity and faith through all vicissitudes of time and fortune; who have been overthrown, crushed, scattered; who have been ground, as it were, to very dust, and flung to the four winds of heaven; yet who, though thrones have fallen, and empires have perished, and creeds have changed, and living tongues have become dead, still exist with a vitality seemingly unimpaired; a people who unite the strangest contradictions; whose annals now blaze with glory, now sound the depths of shame and woe—the advent of such a people marks an epoch in the history of the world.' (Henry George.)

-Akdomus: Translation of a thought at the beginning of *Akdomus*, the Aramaic hymn that precedes the Reading of the Law on Pentecost. I have not been able to discover the name of the translator.

-Rosenfeld: From a forthcoming book of poems, *Songs of a Pilgrim* (Jewish Forum Publishing Co., New York). He is known to the non-Jewish world by his *Songs from the Ghetto*—powerful descriptions of the New York sweatshop inferno. This volume has been translated into most Western languages. 'It was left for a Russian Jew at the end of the nineteenth century to see and paint hell in colours not attempted by anyone since the days of Dante ... the hell he has not only visited, but that he has lived through.' (Wiener.)

-*The Sinaist*, 1, 2. 'The Torah—our Greatest Benefactor.'

-*The Sinaist*, 1, 3.

TEPHILLIN
Erect he stands, in fervent prayer,
His body cloaked in silken Tallis;
He seems a king, so free from care,
His wife a queen, his home a palace.
These bands he wears and softly prays,
Devoting strength and mind to God;
His body slowly, gently sways—
He walks the ground his fathers trod.
This daily commune with the Master
Lifts him above mere common clay;
The Jewish heart, like alabaster,
Grows pure and purer every day.

(Aaron Schaffer in *Standard Book of Jewish Verses*, New York,
 Dodd, Mead & Co.)

-*Sun and Shield*—a book of devout thoughts for everyday use.
Bloch Publishing Co., New York.

-*The Occident*, vol. 12. It is a pity that no selection of S. R.
Hirsch's Essays has as yet appeared in English.

-*Sermons*, I. 'Faith', the last sermon preached by him. The Jewish
idea of faith is that of fidelity, absolute loyalty to God. 'Though He
slay me, yet will I trust in Him.'

-Young Sorley, writing a few days before he fell in battle, says:
'Real faith is not that which says "we *must* win for our cause is just";
but that which says "our cause is just; therefore we can disregard
defeat". All outlooks are at present material, and the unseen value of
justice as justice, independent entirely of results, is forgotten. It is
looked upon merely as an agent for winning battles.' (*Letters of
Charles Sorley*, 1919.)

-Halevi's Ode to Zion is one of the noblest religious poems in the
literature of the World:—

Pure and faithful, ever spotless,
Was his song, even as his soul was;
Soul, that when the Maker fashioned,
With His handiwork delighted.
Straight He kissed the beauteous spirit;
And that kiss of grace, re-echoing,
Fills with music all his singing,
Whom it consecrated—poet.   (Heine.)

-For Israel Baalshem, See Schechter, *Studies*, i. 'The Chassidim.'

-Joseph: *The Message of Judaism.*

-*Songs of Zion.* An excellent translation of a poem of great mystic
beauty.

-This hymn forms part of the New Year Morning Service.

-*Stories and Pictures.* Peretz inimitably succeeds in revealing the
whole inner world of Chassidic life. The Rebbe referred to is Nathan
ben Naphtali Hertz, a disciple of Nahman of Bratzlav. The story is also
related of R. Moses Sassow.

-From a Sermon preached at Capetown to a Congregation of Refugees from the Transvaal during the Boer War.

-*Service of the Synagogue*, Eve of the Day of Atonement. Only the last portion of this alphabetic acrostic is given here.

-From *The Royal Crown*, Gabirol's best known and most important composition, containing his thoughts on religion and philosophy, and expressing all his ardent love of God. In many congregations, this poem is recited at the conclusion of the Eve of Atonement (Kol Nidra) Service.

-*Abodath Yisrael*, by Szold and Jastrow, Philadelphia, 1873.

-*Poems of Emma Lazarus*, vol. II.

-This hymn introduces the concluding service on the Day of Atonement in the Sephardi Liturgy.

-*Cusari*, II, 50. The translation is from Gottheil, *Sun and Shield*.

-Joseph: *Judaism as Life and Creed*.

-Disraeli: *Tancred*.

-*Aspects of Judaism*, p. 109.

-J. Q. R., 1903. For the Yiddish original, See Wiener, *History*, p. 272.

-The Menorah—the more correct title would be 'The Chanukah Lamp'.

-In England every morning service closes with this hymn being recited before the open Ark.

V

-Spinoza: *Ethics*.

-*Guide to the Perplexed*.

-Maimonides: *The Eight Chapters on Ethics*, ed. Gorfinkle, New York, 1912.

-Jacobs: *Jews of Angevin England*, p. 172.

-Ethics of the Fathers: *Authorized Prayer Book*, pp. 184-209. A good edition, Hebrew and English, with commentary, is by Gorfinkle, in Library of Jewish Classics, Bloch Publishing Co., New York.

-'Cleanliness is next to Godliness': The Jewish mystic's Ladder of Perfection. Its author is Rabbi Pinhas ben Yair—a second-century saint and teacher.

-Yellin-Abrahams' *Maimonides*, J. P. S.

-*The Literary Remains of Emanuel Deutsch*, 'The Talmud', for a larger selection of Talmudic sayings.

-*The Discipline of Sorrow*, 1911. 'The terrible events of life are great eye-openers. They force us to learn that which it is wholesome for us to know, but which habitually we try to ignore, namely, that really we have no claim on a long life; that we are each of us liable to be called off at any moment, and that the main point is not how long we live, but with what meaning we fill the short allotted span—for short it is at best.

As in every battle, so in the great battle of Humanity, the fallen and wounded, too, have a share in the victory; by their sufferings they have helped, and the greenest wreaths belong to them.' (Felix Adler in *Life and Destiny*, New York. McClure, Philips & Co.)

-*Aspects of Judaism*, II, 5.

-Adler: 'Baron Ferdinand de Rothschild—a Funeral Address'.

-Penini: translation in Gottheil, *Sun and Shield*.

-'The Jewels'—based on a version by S. T. Coleridge.

-Cf. *Authorized Prayer Book*, p. 318.

-Ethics of the Fathers: The fourth chapter ends with the words of R. Eleazar Hakkappar:—

'The born are to die and the dead to live on again; and those who enter the eternal life, to be judged. Therefore, let it be known, understood and remembered, that He, the Almighty, is the Maker and the Creator; He is the Discerner, He the Judge, He the Witness, He the Complainant; and that He shall judge in the hereafter, before whom there is no unrighteousness, and no forgetting, no regard for rank, no taking of bribes. Know that all is according to reckoning. Let not thy passions persuade thee that the grave will be a place of refuge for thee. For without thy will wert thou created, without thy will thou wast born; thou livest perforce, and perforce thou shalt at last die, and perforce thou shalt in the future have to give account before the Supreme King, the Holy One, blessed be He.'

Ingram Content Group UK Ltd.
Milton Keynes UK
UKHW021112030523
421135UK00003B/24